A THOUSAND AND ONE HAPPY THOUGHTS

to Inspire the Soul

HANAA HAMAD

A THOUSAND AND ONE HAPPY THOUGHTS TO INSPIRE THE SOUL
Copyright © 2015 by Hanaa Hamad

All rights reserved. Printed in the United States of America. No part of this book may be used or reproduced, copied, stored or transmitted in any form or by any means (graphic, electronic, or mechanical, including photocopying, recording, or information storage and retrieval systems) without written permission except in the case of brief quotations em- bodied in critical articles or reviews.

For more information contact:
Hanaa@1001happythoughts.com
Or visit http://www.hanaahamad.com

Book and Cover design by Jovie Camarce
ISBN: 978-0-692-60408-3

First Edition: December 2015

10 9 8 7 6 5 4 3 2 1

For Baba

CONTENTS

INTRODUCTION
THE LAW OF ATTRACTION AND ENERGY 5

ONE
HAPPY THOUGHTS ON THE SELF 60

TWO
RANDOM HAPPY THOUGHTS ON LIFE 87

THREE
HAPPY THOUGHTS ON GOD 116

FOUR
HAPPY THOUGHTS ON FAMILY 123

FIVE
HAPPY THOUGHTS ON LOVE 134

SIX
HAPPY THOUGHTS ON MARRIAGE 142

SEVEN

HAPPY THOUGHTS ON TRAVEL 153

EIGHT
HAPPY THOUGHTS ON FOOD AND EATING 162

NINE
HAPPY THOUGHTS ON MONEY 174

TEN
HAPPY QUOTES BY HAPPY PEOPLE 182

ACKNOWLEDGEMENTS

I wish to thank first, my father, who has fostered my education throughout and for his constant support and encouragement.

To my mom, for always being proud of me and for being the best example in my life of a positive and kind person. And to my grandfather, whose legacy of good energy lives on in our spirits.

I would like to express my deepest appreciation to my husband Ghanem. Thank you so much for taking my word for it and for supporting Zachariah and I throughout.

Thank you to my sisters, Tahany and Jenan, for their unconditional love and support and for their photographic contributions to this project.

Thank you to my brothers, Nadeem and Adam, for their constant encouragement and guidance. Thank you Adam for quickly finding a graphic designer for this project on such short notice. And a special thank you to our friend Jovie Camarce for designing my amazing book cover so promptly.

Thank you to my big family for all the love and support for this project. And my sincerest thank you to all the master spiritual teachers of our time and of the past for inspiring me with this knowledge. For the knowledge you have shared, I am overwhelmed with gratitude.

Introduction

The Law of Attraction and Energy

EVERYTHING GREAT AND everything miraculous has only ever begun with a thought. It has only ever been an idea. That idea was cultivated with absolute conviction, utter faith, and passionate vision. And because of that, it materialized and became reality. Because of that, it became alive.

Buddha once said: "All that we are, is the result of what we have thought." Many of us live our whole lives without ever realizing the power of a thought, or the power of the mind and spirit. Of belief and faith.

The purpose of this book is to teach readers how to live a life of focused and intentional thought. How to think healthy thoughts instead of dysfunctional ones and how important healthy thoughts are to your well-being. It will teach you how to intentionally create the life that you want for yourself through your own empowering thoughts. It will show you the power of your own thinking, and how to gain control of your mind. So, in order for you to become a healthy, happy and successful individual, you must start with your mind. All else stems from there.

At the core of every human thing we seek are three fundamental values: **validation, freedom and joy**. We can trace every desire back to these three roots. We want to know that we matter to those in our lives, that we are seen, that we are heard and understood, that we are loved unconditionally. When we seek things like financial stability, space and distance, what we are really after is freedom. And when seek to change our external circumstances, what we really want to experience is true joy. We believe that if we can change our external world according to our desires, we can discover true joy. But that is not the case. We can find joy despite our circumstances and this book will explain how. I choose the term joy because it means more than happiness—that all is well no matter the circumstances. The healthy thoughts that will follow this chapter will guide you in achieving these three things.

Changing the way you think can improve your health and that is the ultimate message behind this book. My intention behind writing this compilation of happy, healthy thoughts is so that it might bring joy and bliss to all its readers. Once I learned about the law of attraction and energy, I decided to collect all of my positive thoughts in this book so that I would never forget them; they would serve as daily reminders.

In doing so, I took every negative thought I had, found the opposite positive thought and wrote it down, so that I could become accustomed to these happy thoughts rather than the negative ones. This way, the happier thoughts would become more frequent than the upsetting ones, in turn creating a positive consciousness and happier circumstances. Anytime negative thoughts return to my mind, I can deflect them with these positive ones. To all who find yourselves feeling burdened or sad, my hopes are that this book will teach you how to turn the negative thoughts that cause your sadness or your fear into the polar opposite of them...

Happy ones.

This book is not only a collection of positive thoughts, but it is also a collection of convictions or affirmations—affirmations that will guide you to your life's dreams and ambitions. The purpose of these affirmations is to create thought vibrations and the energy of conviction, of doubtlessness and confidence, and of general motivation. They allow us to convince ourselves of our own success, and create an inner energy of motivation and activeness. These affirmations provide us with determination and willingness. But most importantly, they create an energy that attracts back to us the positive circumstances we need to accomplish our goals.

Affirming something to oneself is being certain of that something. That is why saying these affirmations out loud repetitively, and believing in them, feeling that they are real life, creates them as your reality, or real life circumstances and changes your life circumstances. In doing this, we can **speak things into existence. We have the ability to speak things into existence through our energy frequencies.** When we are convinced about that certain something, we manifest it through those thoughts of conviction. This is why reciting affirmations is a beneficial exercise, which is what I ask of all of you as you read these happy thoughts. Doing so also leads to positive feelings and emotions. It creates positive, happy energy. That is how you know you are giving off the right energy to attract the things you want in life.

Some of these thoughts may not apply to your own desires and life. Some may be exactly the thoughts you would like to be thinking. And some may just serve as little reminders for you.

It is imperative that you read these thoughts as absolute fact, or they will not become your reality. What is important about these happy thoughts is not simply thinking them alone but believing in them as well, because if you believe in these thoughts as your current reality, if you act, speak and live as if these thoughts are real, they become your reality in actuality. Yes, I realize that to most people, this sounds absolutely farfetched at first, and you are probably thinking, how is that possible? Allow me to complete my explanation.

What I am referring to is the law of attraction and affirmative energy. These two things have the ability to completely turn your life around, from unbearable misery to absolute happiness. I know, it sounds too good to be true, but this time it actually is not.

Many of us have heard or read about the law of attraction at some point in our lives. The law of attraction states that like attracts like. This means that things that are alike attract one another. For example, we are all attracted to people with similar interests or "likes" as ourselves. This phrase also means that things perpetuate, and that whatever our focus is, we attract more of, or like it.

You might be wondering how this law of attraction works. It is actually a very simple concept.

Energy.

At our deepest core, and beyond our physical bodies, we are all simply energy. Whatever kind of energy we give off determines our life's outcomes. That energy can be positive or negative. Every living thing in the universe has energy. No one can deny that. The universe is also energy. No one can deny that either. But what most people are not aware of is that everything that is energy emits a frequency. This means that you, your mind and your body, emits an energy frequency. And this frequency begins with your thoughts.

Charles Haanel once stated: "The vibrations of mental forces are the finest and consequently the most powerful in existence." He was referring to the idea that your thoughts and your emotions create your energy, and create your energy frequency, or vibrations. This means that whatever kind of energy, frequency, or vibrations you are emitting attracts the like back to you. If you are emitting positive energy out into the world, then you are attracting back positive circumstances. But if you are emitting negative energy out into the world, then you are attracting back to yourself negative circumstances and outcomes. The most amazing thing about the universe is that it responds to your energy frequency and reflects back to you what you think of yourself and what you think of your life at all times. It never stops this motion. It is an infinite, ongoing process. As Lisa Nichols in *The Secret* puts it: "It's working as much as you're thinking. Anytime your thoughts are flowing, the law of attraction is operational. When you're thinking about the past, the present, or the future, the law of attraction is working... It is forever in action, as your thoughts are."

It is always responding to our dominant thoughts and creating our life circumstances based off of our energy frequencies.

James Arthur Ray in *The Secret* states: "Most people define themselves by this finite body, but you're not a finite body. Even under a microscope, you're an energy field...You're an energy field operating in a larger energy field." I'm sure we can all agree that we are not simply bodies.

Quantum Physics substantiates these ideas. The commonly understood mass energy equivalence equation,

$E = MC^2$, formulated by Albert Einstein, has much to do with this philosophy. The letter E in the formula represents Energy, M represents mass and C represents the speed of light. This formula demonstrates how energy and the body are relative to one another. That the mass of a body can be measured based on its energy content and that our bodies give off energy.

So, for anyone who believes in the mind body relationship, or spirituality, or the miraculous existence of the soul, believe in the energy of it. Your soul has energy.

This law of attraction is a tool that God has blessed us with, in alignment and connection with Him, it is infinite like Him, and it is part of the free will that he's blessed us with. He has given us the freedom of choice and creation and this is the tool He's blessed us with to do so, and to do His work on earth.

Before this discovery, I found that one of the most painfully wrenching parts about being a human is the inevitable reunion with uncertainty. But once you know the power of thought and energy, you can eliminate the pain of uncertainty from your life forever. Never again must you be afraid of the unknown. Because now you know that your beliefs are what makes things certain and are what makes your reality. Know that your fear is not really real at all. It is only as real as you make it.

The message I'm giving you in this book is not simply that all things are possible, because yes, the law of gravity tells us that what goes up must come down, and yes, all living beings will eventually die, but I believe that miracles truly exist. I believe that bad circumstances can become the opposite of what they had been. I believe that there are ways to make impossible things possible, ways that we have not yet conceived of. I believe that the world is full of possibilities.

And perhaps you are thinking that this world can't possibly bring every person everything they want. But think twice. Think about how miraculous the universe already is. The world is already incredibly resourceful, and is constantly producing more and more. The abundance of water and oceans are miraculous, the existence of human beings is miraculous, the sky is miraculous, so why would an abundance of resources for everyone be impossible? Why couldn't this miraculous world produce more than enough for everyone? Why couldn't it be more miraculous? If there is room for these miraculous things in the world, then there is room for plenty more.

As you are processing this information, you might be feeling skeptical about a lot of it. This is a natural reaction anytime a new idea is presented to anyone. For example, when you explain your religion to someone who is not of that faith, they first think it strange, and do not understand or relate to it. It takes elaboration and good explanation to get someone to understand a philosophy or belief. Let's say you were not born the religion you are now. Someone walks up to you and explains your religion to you. Would you immediately be accepting of it? Most likely not, because we have all been taught not to be fooled. We often try to protect ourselves from falsehood, so we close off our minds and our hearts. But if we open them up just a little bit, not to the point of being naïve, we can begin to understand and believe in many things, because we are all capable of believing in anything.

What makes it so difficult for most people to believe in optimism and the law of attraction is the fear of failure, and the fear of being vulnerable, which is very limiting for many reasons. Not only does fear prevent us from taking risks and daring to achieve, but it is also is a type of negative energy. Fear is the energy of all misfortune. Doubt, which stems from fear, is also what makes people resistant to optimism. They doubt that they can fulfill their dreams therefore, they refuse to be optimistic in order to protect themselves from the pain of failure. But what they do not realize is that failure is a part of their journey. Without the risk of failure, we accomplish nothing. If we want to achieve, we must be willing to fail. We must dare greatly, as Roosevelt said. We must be willing to be vulnerable. And in our journeys, if we continue to try with determination and faith, that failure will eventually become success, because our belief will guide us until we get there. Michael Jordan, known as the greatest basketball player who ever lived, stated: "I've failed over and over and over again in my life. And that is why I succeed." We have to remember that sometimes when we fail, it is a necessary step in our journey to accomplishment.

In order to achieve well being and success, it takes the mastering of three major concepts: **Consciousness, Affirmation and Gratitude.**

Simply becoming aware, affirming positive thoughts to yourself and feeling gratitude is how you can begin to draw more happiness into your life. These three concepts are the key tools needed when using the law of attraction.

If you're still having trouble understanding the law of attraction, think of this law in comparison to the placebo effect. When you take a sugar pill unknowingly, and you are under the assumption that it is the solution to your illness, it actually cures you. Why? Because you believed it would. You were certain that it was the cure. What I am asking of you, the reader, is to apply this placebo concept to your active life.

How do we go about doing that?

We can start with our awareness. There are four things that we can begin to become aware of and four things we can begin to take control of. Those are our:

1. Thoughts

2. Feelings

3. Actions

4. Words

CONSCIOUSNESS

Thoughts and Feelings

OUR INTERNAL WORLD, our internal being has everything to do with our overall well-being and with our wholeness; the mind plays the most important part in both our internal world and external world. It is what determines our external world and our physical circumstances. What comprises our inner being are two fundamental things: our mind and our spirit. The well being of the spirit, of the soul, is determined by the mind. And when the mind is positive, so will be the spirit. Once you have learned about the power of the mind and spirit combination you can begin to change your life dramatically. Once you have mastered your mind, the wellness of your spirit will stem from there.

Our entire sense of consciousness begins with our mind, and our mind determines the emotions we feel and the overall wellness of our spirit. Therefore, if we can begin to become more aware of our thoughts, we can begin to feel well. If we choose to think healthy thoughts, it will affect our spirit and our entire being, as well as our external world. We will draw in positive circumstances and create a better living situation.

Henry Ford once made the statement: "whether you think you can, or think you can't, either way, you are right." By this he meant that the perception of something is what you think it is. As Dr. Robert Holden, author and psychologist, puts it, whatever our beliefs are, whatever our perception is, "we will gather evidence to prove to ourselves" that our perceptions are true. In addition to that, the law of attraction will show us that our beliefs and perceptions are true. For example, if you perceive your spouse to be unfaithful, then you will attract circumstances that will show you that your spouse is unfaithful, whether your spouse is faithful or not. You will also find evidence to prove this to yourself, small evidence or large evidence, and you will focus on this infidelity (whether it is real or not), therefore, you will attract it into your life. But, if you believe your spouse is loyal, then you will attract circumstances that show you that your spouse is loyal and you will gather evidence that proves that to yourself. Focusing on the loyalty will attract more of it into your life.

We all tend to perceive our problems as large, therefore it becomes a large part of our lives, but once we realize how small our problems really are (how much worse things could be) we can begin to eliminate these problems from our lives. All we need is a shift in our perception.

Some might argue that these philosophies might deter someone from their own reality and create false hope. But what they fail to realize is that nothing is ever real unless we perceive it to be. The mind cannot distinguish between reality and imagination unless we decide for it to do so. Whatever we perceive to be real is real, and all else is illusion. Therefore, fear is never real unless you decide for it to be real. It only exists because we allow it to exist in our minds and our spirits. We ourselves have created it, just as we have drawn in all else in our lives.

However this does not mean that you should suppress your fear, or any humanly emotion you are feeling, whether it is sadness, anger, or grief. You are a human being and you have the right to feel all of your humanly emotions. If you suppress your emotions, this traps them within you, and they settle within your subconscious. They will eventually surface as explosive or bad behaviors and you will not be aware of what is truly bothering you. Suppressing your emotions creates a density in your being, and does not allow you to grow from your emotional experiences. When pain finds you, recognize what is causing your suffering and allow yourself to feel and release it. Then you are able to let it pass through you and let it go. Without embracing it, you can never let it go. If you are feeling afraid and doubtful, embrace that fear. Recognize the fear and the doubt and replace them with love and trust. That is how you can eliminate them. Accept all of your emotions as a state of being; become aware of them and then release them. Surrender them to God, and trust with absolute certainty that whatever pain has befallen you has a greater purpose. It has happened to you in order to take you somewhere greater. In order to teach you something you did not know. In order to prepare you, to make you better and to make you more whole. Allow yourself to see the bigger picture of your life or to trust that there is one, even if you can't picture it or understand it yet. Once you have allowed yourself to feel your emotions, you can release them and begin to refocus on all of your goals. You can then make a new choice and create a new train of thought that stems from love, trust and joy. Going through this process is how you can ultimately cultivate your spirit and come to a state of well-being.

Perhaps your unfair circumstances are real in your outer world, but they never have to be real within you unless you decide for them to be. They are only your current circumstances, not your future. If you so chose, your current circumstances can be the illusion. And whatever is real in your mind becomes real in your life. Our inner reality can be separated from our outer reality and we can decide which reality is our own truth. Whatever is within our inner reality will always become our outer reality. We always have the choice to decide what is real to us and what is not. We always have the ability to create our own reality. Often times, when we perceive things the way we want to, our inner reality becomes controlled by our emotions; in truth, we create these emotions ourselves by assuming negatively and believing what we want to believe. Whatever we choose to believe will cultivate itself within our inner reality and therefore will create those emotions and those realities.

When your inner reality is being cultivated by your negative emotions, you will soon be heading down a sorry path. Your emotions are only real because you chose to believe in a certain thought. You always have the power to think a new thought and to redesign your inner reality. Reality is what we believe it to be, so when we create negative assumptions and beliefs about others and ourselves, we create negative emotions and a negative reality by believing it all to be real.

Success in life is all about mind control, and by that I mean controlling your own mind. If you can control your mind, then you can control your life and you will have the ability to guide yourself to success.

Most people believe that in order to feel true happiness, they must fulfill their next goal or ambition. They hold in their consciousness that they cannot be happy until they have accomplished this goal, therefore keeping their joy at a distance. What they do not realize is that they do not need to have arrived at their next goal in order to feel happy. They can feel happy now. They can become present and begin to feel grateful for all the amazing things they already have. They can embrace their lives as they are now rather than continuing to resist them. In fact, that only draws in more of the same circumstances. They can also begin celebrating the fulfillment of the goal that they are in pursuit of. If we celebrate accomplishing our goals in the present moments, we can attract our goals at a faster rate. If we feel the joy of accomplishment now, it will become now. If we celebrate in the present, all that we want to celebrate will become present. However, if we keep telling ourselves that we can only feel happy once we have accomplished our goals, then we can never actually arrive at that happiness, because we would still be perceiving it to be in the distance, therefore, it will always remain in the distance and we will never draw it into our lives. Remember, perception is everything, so we must begin to perceive with absolute confidence that we have already accomplished our goals and most importantly, we must begin to feel joyful and blissful now. We must begin a new awareness. Pastor Joel Osteen says: "If you're not happy where you are, you probably won't get to where you want to be." We cannot find happiness until we have learned to appreciate what we already have to be thankful for, and to be happy with our lives as they are now.

When we are aware of our emotions, then we can also become aware of where our emotions are coming from, and that is our thoughts. Our emotions are created by our thoughts; therefore when we're having bad thoughts, we will feel bad emotions as well. And if we're having good thoughts, we will have good emotions. When we're feeling bad, we can realize that it is because we're thinking bad thoughts; then we know that we must change our current thinking and we know where the bad emotions are coming from. This is how we can use our emotions to show us what we are thinking.

Let's become more familiar with positive and negative emotions. This will help with the awareness process, and also help you recognize your energy frequency.

Positive emotions are: joy, gratitude, bliss, praise, appreciation and satisfaction. Relaxation or meditation can also help create a positive energy frequency, and produce emotions like calmness and serenity (we will further discuss meditation later in this introduction).

Negative emotions are: resentment, hopelessness, guilt, anger, frustration and fear. Feeling a lack of time is also a negative emotion, and creates the act of rushing. When we are rushing, we feel the lack of time, therefore we create more of it. The way to counter this is to always think, "I have more than enough time." The lack of time, if felt frequently, can also become a part of our subconscious. When it is within our subconscious, we must bring it to our consciousness and put a halt to it, because it can lead to worse circumstances, and possibly, fatal illnesses due to the fact that we feel the lack of time when death approaches. If we are constantly feeling the lack of time, we are drawing death in, because death is the ultimate signifier of having no time left.

Knowing our emotions is how we can differentiate good energy from bad energy. Thoughts, feelings, actions and words that make you feel good lead to a positive energy frequency, while thoughts, feelings, actions and words that make you feel bad lead to a negative energy frequency.

Ultimately, you must be feeling good in order to be sending out positive frequencies into the universe. You must feel the feelings of joy, bliss and happiness as you read these happy thoughts. You must feel as if these thoughts are your reality. The reason I chose to write many of these thoughts in the past tense is to allow the reader to feel that they have already achieved these happy thoughts. Keep in mind that your emotions carry more weight than your thoughts and have stronger vibrations or quantum wave functions. Your emotions deeply affect your energy levels and are tremendously powerful, because they determine the speed at which the outcomes of our energy manifest. Your emotions can draw things into your life at a faster rate. So you must be very aware of your emotions as well as your thoughts.

Passion becomes key to this part of the practice. Passion is emotion at its highest level. And the more we are feeling passionately content or passionately discouraged, the faster we attract more contentment or discouragement. Being passionately afraid of something is how you draw in that which you are afraid of. This is why our thoughts are crucial and beneficial to us. When we control our thoughts, we can control our emotions as well, because our thoughts create our emotions. If our thoughts are happy, then our emotions will be too. So it is very important to remember that our feelings stem from our thoughts, which is why we must be aware of what we are thinking about.

Anytime you are in a situation where you are feeling hopeless about the circumstances of your life, and you are constantly thinking about your negative circumstances and feeling depressed, incapable and doubtful, you need to stop right there. Completely halt your thoughts, and think about the polar opposite of those circumstances, and all that is upsetting you. For example, let's say your current circumstances are that you and your husband/wife disagree about having children. Your husband/wife is not ready for children while you are; you feel hopeless.

The best way to approach this issue is to stop thinking hopeless thoughts, because you are only attracting more of that hopelessness. Instead of feeling intensely depressed, feel intensely joyous by imagining yourself with the children you want to have. Imagine your husband or wife being happy with your future children, and do this frequently. Your partner will most likely have a change of heart sooner than you think. Somehow, someway, you both will come to a happy compromise. Feel that satisfaction, that relief, and that bliss! This is called affirmative thinking. Start thinking about all the magnificent things you have asked God for, and get excited that you will have them all very, very soon.

If that is too difficult, start off with a gratitude journal. Start thanking God for the things you already have, and then move into affirmative thinking. Gratitude is a great way to turn a bad mood into an uplifting one. If you find yourself feeling afraid, begin writing down the things you are grateful for. Gratitude eliminates fear. It is also a major tool when using the law of attraction. Something I always say to everyone I know is this: "You have so much to be grateful for." Because it is always true. No matter your circumstances, you always have something and you can always be thankful for it. You have the ability to walk. You have the ability to see. To taste. To hear. To smell. To laugh. You have time. You have breath in your lungs. You are alive. Start with the simplest of blessings. The blessings that everyone can be thankful for. You can begin to look around you and find all the things you are grateful for in life. The big things and the little things. Be grateful for your television set, for your toilet, for you health. Or for your bed, for your couch, for your soft carpet. Write them down in a journal. This allows you to focus on these thoughts and put more good energy into them; it allows you to spend more time with these thoughts. Appreciate everything in your life, and become present in each moment. Become conscious of all of your blessings. This is how you will be blessed with more. Your energy frequency will attract more.

Prayer is incredibly relative to the concept of energy. Prayer is energy. When you pray, you are sending out energy through your prayer. This makes prayer a great tool for attracting the things you want and need. It is also why God asks us to pray. Not because He needs our prayer, but because we need our prayer. We need Him. God has given us the gift of prayer as a means of sending out our energy so that we may receive. Never underestimate the power of your prayer and the energy you send to God. When your faith is unwavering, God will respond without waver. So ask God for your desires, but with celebration that they have already arrived. "Feel the joy rising," as Oprah Winfrey says.

Something you must always remember is, never focus on what you do not want, because it is going to make you feel terrible and you will attract more of what is making you feel terrible. It seems that we are a culture that chooses to focus on the scarcity or lack of things within our lives. We focus on the lack of time, sleep, beauty, money and so on. Instead, try focusing on what you do want and what you already have. Feel the abundance in your life and all that you have to be grateful for. Feel good. Feel great! And you will attract more of that instead.

Sometimes, we anticipate problems that have not even come into existence; we anticipate them even though they are far away. By doing this, we welcome trouble ahead of time, therefore trouble arrives. But if we anticipate success and joy, then that is what we will receive.

For example, when good things happen to us, we tend to fear that we will lose those good things, because we put so much of our energy and focus into those things in order to gain them. These desires that we have already attained have become the most important thing to us; therefore if we were to lose them, we would lose everything. This creates fear and negative energy, which attracts that loss through the fear of it. That is how we are constantly breaking the good chain and re-starting a bad one. If loss does come our way and we lose something or someone that had been of great value to us, we must remember the great visions we have for our lives or understand that a bigger picture exists. We must trust that everything that occurs in our lives holds a greater, deeper, important purpose. The times we feel loss at its deepest are the times we forget our greatest visions.

Have you ever listened to someone who complains all the time and wondered why their life was so terrible and why things were always going badly for them? It is because they have maintained a negative way of thinking and a negative energy frequency. Their subconscious mind and inner spirituality has grown accustomed to negativity. Or perhaps they live busy lives in which they are constantly feeling scarcity, always rushing, always feeling a lack of time, or never make time for themselves. They don't make time for relaxation, reflection or meditation; therefore, they lose focus of their goals and desires. When we do not make time for ourselves, and when we are in a constant state of rush, we are creating a scarcity mindset of "the lack of" and a negative energy frequency, in turn creating more and more of the lack of something.

It is also very dangerous to constantly live as if we are running out of time, because again, we draw more of the lack of time into our lives, and that can manifest in the form of cancer or illness or depleting health. The feeling of a lack of time is also what creates stress, and stress has always been the greatest cause of bad health and disease.

Our lives are so fast paced. And we act on that. We move quickly and continuously in that fashion, drawing more busyness into our lives. The way to counter this cycle is simply to slow down. Stop rushing through each daily event as if you are running out of time. Move slower as if you have the time to spare. This is how you can draw infinite free time into your life.

If you are still not convinced about the law of attraction, think back to all the times bad things have happened to you. Didn't things always get worse and worse as you grew more and more frustrated? It always ties back to your level of emotion and how passionately you are feeling.

Meditation and Visual Motor Rehearsal

MANY OF US are so busy each day that we don't even realize that we haven't taken the time to reflect on our lives and what is going on within us. We also do not realize that reflection is what is going to make everything better. When we reflect on our thoughts and emotions, we can begin to understand what is bothering us not only in our consciousness, but what has been suppressed within our subconscious as well and we can bring that forth into our conscious thought. Once we have figured out what is bothering us, we can turn the negative thoughts and emotions into positive ones.

Fantasizing and visualizing are great ways to lift your spirit and stop a negative thought downward spiral. When you find yourself tired of waiting for your desires to manifest, go there in your mind and visualize living it right now. The subconscious mind does not differentiate between reality and imagination, so you will be able to truly feel as though these visions are real, whether they are or not, and that's what's important. Our minds respond to the images that we have in them, and the images that we choose to have. Within each fantasy are numerous happy thoughts that create strong positive frequencies. Specify each happy thought, see every fantasy exactly how you want it, down to every detail. Try creating a vision board using pictures of the things you want, and use these pictures to help you see your desires. Find as many visuals of your desires as you can and look at them or watch them as often as you can. The important thing is that you're feeling passionately happy or satisfied. This will create more positive energy for you and a stronger, faster frequency of joy.

It is important to focus all of your attention or consciousness on these thoughts. For example, let's say you are engaged, and you really want your mother to love your fiancé. Visualize your mother saying how much she loves your fiancé over and over again.

This key exercise is called visual motor rehearsal, which was created for the Apollo mission, and implemented by Dr. Denis Waitley during the 1980's and 1990's Olympics program. It is incredibly beneficial to the positive thinker. Dr. Waitley expressed in the documentary The Secret that "when you visualize, then you materialize." By this he means that what you see and enjoy in your mind will materialize in some form or another into reality. Dr Waitley explains:

"I took the visualization process from the Apollo program, and instituted it during the 1980's and 90's into the Olympic program. It was called Visual Motor Rehearsal. When you visualize then you materialize. Here's an interesting thing about the mind: we took Olympic athletes, and then hooked them up to sophisticated biofeedback equipment, and had them run their event only in their mind. Incredibly, the same muscles fired in the same sequence when they were running the race in their mind as when they were running it on the track. How can this be? Because the mind cannot distinguish whether you're really doing it or whether it's just a practice. I think if you've been there in the mind, you go there in the body."

This is why visualization and meditation are important during the creative process of bringing good things into your life. If we see it, and if we feel the joy of having already acquired it, we can materialize it and it will arrive.

Meditation is a great way to become more conscious and present. It allows us to become conscious of our surroundings, and of our blessings. If we want to get in touch with our spirit, meditation is the key. It is how we can connect with God, our surroundings and our own presence in the world. It brings us to an inner blissful awareness and takes us into our own true inner reality.

It helps us to embrace and accept all of our emotions and all that has happened to us. It allows us to recognize ourselves as we are and our lives as they are, and surrender everything to God, bringing a calm energy into our being. When we're feeling calm, we release the energy of trust, calmness and contentment and draw that into our lives. When we are calm, we demonstrate to God that we are content with our current blessings and that we are confident that His future blessings are on the way. This draws more blessings into our lives. When we are calm, we are sending out the energy of trust in the perfection of our destinies. We demonstrate to God that we trust that He will guide us, and present us with the answers we seek, that we trust in His generosity and His capabilities. And why shouldn't He bless us when we are fully confident in His Grace?

During meditation, we can also visualize having already acquired our desires. If we can begin to imagine that our blessings have already materialized during meditation, then we can create the feeling and frequency of having it now, which in turn creates a faster frequency. It allows us to feel the joys of actually experiencing our desires. And because the mind does not distinguish between reality and imagination, our reality is whatever we perceive it to be. I recommend that you practice the techniques of visual motor rehearsal and meditation in the morning when you wake and at night before you sleep. The reason I suggest these times is because they are nearest to the times that you sleep, and our subconscious does the most work while we sleep. It is very important that you get your vision solidified and settled into your subconscious. The faster you ground this vision into your subconscious, the sooner it will show up in your life. It is also good to try visualizing as frequently as you can. Again, the more often you do it, the stronger and faster your vibrational frequency becomes.

If you have been trying all of these techniques and still find yourself unhappy or dissatisfied about something in your life, it may be that you do not yet have a clear vision of what you truly want. Yes, you may know that you want a new home or infinite space and time for yourself, but you are not really seeing it yet. You need to go inside yourself and imagine it. Live there in that reality, and see it, and feel it, the joy of it rising more and more. This is true visualization. Inspirational speaker Iyanla Vanzant says: "If you don't have a vision, you're going to be stuck in what you know. And the only thing you know is what you've already seen." So I urge you to see something new for yourself. Picture your life exactly the way you want it to be, down to each detail. Create it, then play it like a film in your mind. Watch it over and over and over again. And once you have this vision and you replay it everyday, as often as you can, it will draw nearer and nearer and you will stay happy, even if it hasn't yet arrived. So have a clear vision of the life you want to be living. Wake up in that life every morning. Live it in your mind, hold it within your inner truth, until it becomes your external truth. Once you have the vision, you can carry it with you wherever you go, and you can be in a constant state of joy.

Albert Einstein, who understood the process of visualization, stated something along these lines. He said: "Imagination is everything. It is the preview of life's coming attractions." So I urge you to become a visionary and visualize your life the way you want it to be.

CONSCIOUSNESS

Actions and Words

AS DEEPAK CHOPRA puts it: "Words are patterns of reality making and are the magical property of those who use them wisely."

Not only must we monitor our thoughts and feelings, but we must also bring awareness to our actions and words, and they must be based on our positive thoughts and emotions. We must remember that our words are tremendously powerful, and emit energy. That our words greatly effect the outcomes of our lives.

When you are constantly talking about what you do not want, you end up attracting more of that. For example, if you are constantly saying: "I do not want to get married," then you are attracting marriage. Why? Because you are constantly thinking, talking and feeling marriage, and because marriage is your focus. You are focusing on what you do not want. You are also resisting marriage. Resistance is an action in accordance with negative energy. This is because when you resist something, you are adding energy to it, therefore attracting more of it. When you resist something, you are giving it more power and more existence. Your mere dislike of it makes it more. Carl Jung famously stated: "What you resist, persists." If you apply this statement to anything you've ever resisted in your life, both inwardly and outwardly, you'll find this statement to be true. Mother Theresa said something relative to this idea. She stated: "I was once asked why I don't participate in anti-war demonstrations. I said that I will never do that, but as soon as you have a pro-peace rally, I'll be there." Mother Theresa made this statement because she knew that when you resist war, when you resist terrorism, when you resist pollution, especially as a community in which the energy is collective, you are calling it into being more than it already is. Collective energy from the masses is tremendously powerful, whether it is positive or negative.

If you find yourself in circumstances or situations that you dislike or are uncomfortable with, stop disliking them and embrace them. A well-known Japanese proverb states: "Be like a bamboo; it bends but does not break; it is flexible, yet firmly rooted. The bamboo that bends is stronger than the oak that resists." This simply means that the more you are willing to flow with life, the less negative circumstances you will find yourself revisiting.

In addition to that, if you are focusing on what you do not want, you are also emitting a frequency of the fear of something, therefore, drawing it to you. Remember, when you are feeling the fear of something, you are drawing it in. So if you fear marriage and resist marriage in your inner reality, then you are attracting it into your outer reality as well. You are calling something into being that does not even exist. The only thing that exists is the fear of it in you.

That is also the case if you are speaking positively. The power of the spoken word is very crucial. For example, when you say to yourself, "I am brilliant," you are attracting circumstances that will show you how brilliant you are, and circumstances that will make you feel brilliant as well. In addition, try imagining yourself being brilliant at something, whatever is important to you, whether it may be Chemistry, or writing, or painting, or singing. Imagine people telling you that you are brilliant; imagine people admiring your work, and agreeing with what you say. Sit down and write down as many moments as you can where you did something brilliant in your life, or when someone made you feel brilliant about yourself. This is how you can begin a new train of thought or move into a positive direction. These simple thoughts and memories will create a ripple effect in your thoughts and energy frequency, and in your spirit as a whole.

It is crucial to be very careful about the way we word a thought, and when we're saying that thought out loud as well. When it comes to thought and speech, there are negative words and there are positive words when composing a thought or a sentence. You'll notice that I did not choose any negative words in the composition of these happy thoughts, because there is a very precise way to make a thought or statement a positive one. For example, if you say "I am so happy that I never have to hear complaining," what do you think you'll be attracting?

Complaining!

Because you were thinking complaining. Although it sounds like a positive statement because it is expressing gratitude and happiness, it is not, because the focus is complaining. So, rather than choosing the word complaining, I chose the word "praise" instead. Complain is a negative word. Praise is a positive word. So the best way to word this thought would be: "I am so grateful that I am always being praised."

Have you ever noticed how, when you make statements like, "I never get sick," or, "I never get tired," exactly the opposite happens? It is because you were thinking of what you did not want. The average American would call this jinxing themselves, however, it is nothing of the sort. It is the law of attraction in action. Keep in mind that your spoken words are energy.

Our actions can also help speed up the creative process. It is crucial at times as well. For example, let's say your greatest desire is to get engaged. You've been speaking, visualizing, and thinking like you are already engaged. But it still has not manifested. What's missing?

Action.

Start wearing an engagement ring! It doesn't have to be expensive, and it doesn't even have to be real gold. You just need to experience the feeling of wearing an engagement ring. Hold your hand out and look at it. Feel the joy of being engaged.

If absolute freedom is your desire, then begin to feel freedom during the most ordinary moments of your life. As you read, as you dress yourself, as you brush your teeth and as you do things you enjoy. Affirm out loud to yourself, "I am free, I am free, I am free" and "These moments are mine, these moments are mine, these moments are mine." If money is your desire, then begin by cherishing the fiscal value of your smallest possessions. Shop online as if you had the money. Add things to your shopping cart; you don't have to actually checkout, but add to your shopping cart as if you had the money to buy all the things you have been wanting. Start being grateful for the most ordinary of things and those ordinary things will become extraordinary.

Count your future blessings and they will arrive. In doing so, you're trusting God to such an extent that you're thanking Him ahead of time. Whatever it is you are pursuing, celebrate having it now. Jump up and down. Throw your fists in the air. Throw your arms in the air. Wave them. Shake them. Shout for joy! Feel that joy, feel that excitement, and feel that celebration. All of these actions create intense positive energy and a faster frequency. Why? Because doing so sends out the energy of joy and of absolute faith, therefore, you are drawing it in.

If you feel inspired by a thought, you must act on that inspiration immediately. There is no better time to act than when inspired. If you do not act, the inspiration will die down and you might lose out on an opportunity for happiness. Also, when you receive and feel inspiration, this means that you are in line with a frequency that will lead you to a success. Your inspiration is not coincidence. It is in line with your energy frequency and you need to act on that energy in order to receive. You will also find that the action will feel effortless, because it comes from passion. It will most likely never feel like hard work. You will enjoy it; therefore it will not be difficult (as goals tend to be perceived).

Another way to practice "action-in-accordance-with" is by giving. When you give, you create a vacuum that allows blessings to flow into your life. In other words, you are not only serving others, but you are also serving yourself, God and the universe. And it does not necessarily mean that we should give only material things. We can give by giving others our time, our effort and our assistance. For example, when you give someone some form of freedom, whether that be the freedom of time, the freedom of choice or the freedom of space, you will receive your own freedom. But if you take someone else's freedom, you will find yourself a slave to something or someone. That is the karmic effect of giving and service, or The Law of Karma as it applies to every action we take, positive or negative. The world is here to serve you as you are here to serve it. If you want to receive more, you have to be willing to give. We cannot expect to receive if we

Hamad

are not willing to give.

In sum, speak, act, think and feel positively and stay aware of the power of each of these practices. It takes all four.

How?

One of the most important questions throughout this process is, how? How can I change my circumstances when things are this bad? Most people give up their happiness because they simply cannot see how things can turn around for the better. Because they cannot conceive it, they cannot believe in it.

There is another simple answer to this problem.

Leave the how up to the law of attraction, or up to the universe, or up to God. God has never asked us to figure out the how. He's never told us to search for the answers. God only asks us to believe and to have unwavering faith. He only asks us to trust in Him. God does not bless us with a dream without properly preparing us and guiding us there. You must accept the fact that in the beginning of your journey, you will never know how you will accomplish your goals. This knowledge will always remain with God. All you need to know is that He will guide you, and it will happen. So, believe in the unseen. Say to yourself: "I know my heart will never misguide me, because my heart was created by God Himself." Become still and present. Quiet your mind and breath deep. Listen to your intuition, to your heart. That's God telling you where to go. God will never misguide you, and neither will your intuition. God makes no mistakes. So, begin to learn how to trust in your conviction and in your energy. Begin to trust that wherever you are right now is exactly where you're meant to be. Any mistake, setback or regret is nothing of the sort. They have only ever been blessings in disguise or important steps in your journey. Hafiz, the fourteenth century Persian poet famously stated: "This place where you are right now, God circled on a map for you."

You must remember not to worry about how you will attract what you want as you continue on your journey of achievement. You must simply focus on what it is that you desire most. When you are so busy worrying about how you will accomplish your visions, you give off the energy of doubt and the reality that you have not yet achieved it. Worrying sends out the energy of fear, therefore drawing in negative circumstances and more fear. But in order for your dreams to manifest, you should be giving off the energy of absolute, affirmative confidence that your dreams have already happened and that you have already acquired the things you desire. That they are on their way to you.

That may sound insane at first, but if we turn to history, we might remember that many of the greatest people that have ever done anything phenomenal have never known how they were going to accomplish their goals when they began. Many people perceived these innovators as insane and criticized them, because they could not see how these goals could be manifested. The greatest visionaries like Alexander Graham Bell, Walt Disney, and Thomas Edison did not start out knowing how they were going to accomplish their goals once they had become inspired. They only knew that they were absolutely going to accomplish them, and with this conviction, God and the law of attraction guided them to what they needed, things fell into place, and miraculously, they found a way for creation to occur. As Michael Beckwith puts it, "out of nothing, and out of no way, a way will be made." After all, was the universe not created from nothing?

Jack Canfield, author and creator of the Chicken Soup for the Soul series, explains this idea further in the following passage from *The Secret*:

"Think of this. A car driving through the night, the headlights only go a hundred to two hundred feet forward, and you can make it all the way from California to New York, driving through the dark, because all you have to see is the next two hundred feet. That's how life tends to unfold before us, and if we just trust that the next two hundred feet will unfold after that and the next two hundred feet will unfold after that, your life will keep unfolding and it will eventually get you to the destination of whatever it is that you truly want, because you want it."

Steve Jobs, the innovative creator of the Apple Company, also understood the philosophy of trusting your energy frequency and God. In his famous speech at Harvard, he stated:

"You can't connect the dots looking forward; you can only connect them looking backwards. So you have to trust that the dots will somehow connect in your future. You have to trust in something — your gut, destiny, life, karma, whatever. This approach has never let me down, and it has made all the difference in my life."

If you believe in God, believe in His capabilities. Know that He is capable of bringing you anything you want. Your faith must be unfaltering, because why should God bless you if you are not absolutely certain that He will? Pastor Joel Osteen says: "God meets you at the level of your expectations. If you don't expect much, if you pray little, you believe little, you're going to receive little."

When you ask God for something, hold no doubt in your heart. Never think: perhaps God will bless me with what I'm asking Him for, and perhaps He will not. Because if you hold any doubt in your heart when you are asking God for something, then you are telling God that you not only doubt His Mercy, but His Generosity, His Capabilities and His Love as well. You will give off a frequency of doubt, it will grow deeper in your life, and you will bring more of it into your life. Your desires will not manifest because your mind and your energy will keep you in limbo. When you love and appreciate God, He will always be on your side. When you are grateful to God, He will always bless you with more. And when you ask God for something, be absolutely certain that He will answer you positively. Because when you believe with unfaltering faith that God will bless you, He will make a way. A way that you are not yet able to conceive of.

You don't have to remain sad. You don't have to remain afraid. God is truly with you, and God will give you the answers when you are in need of His guidance. Feel Him in your spirit whenever you are sad or afraid, feel the power of His Love and you will feel confident again. Whatever it is that you are afraid of, God can stop it. He is always Greater than it.

To put it simply: choose happiness. We often think that things are not in our control, but they are. Yes, we may not have complete control over our lives at all times, but what we do have control over is the ability to choose our thoughts and we will always have that choice. That free will is the greatest tool that God has given us. We have control over what we think and how we feel. All we have to do is choose our thoughts, emotions, actions and words wisely. All we have to do is choose healthy thoughts, because life is what we think it is. If we think life is hard, then it will be just that. And if we think life is spectacular, then it will be that too. Whatever the circumstances, everything is always what we perceive it to be.

Each day, create small victories in your life. If you completed a task or an assignment or a chore, celebrate that, and enjoy your free time. That is how you will attract more. Look deeper for the beautiful things in your life, and appreciate them. Feel that appreciation intensely, feel that joy. This could be anything, from the appreciation of your spouse, to your health, to your legs, your hearing, and your vision. Perhaps you have beautiful hands, perhaps you have beautiful eyes, and perhaps you have beautiful lips. Appreciate that beauty.

Some people wonder, how can we make ourselves happy when we simply cannot feel happiness? If ever you are upset, one simple way to do this is to think of all the blessings you have. Then think, what if I lost all of them tomorrow? How would I feel? Imagine for a second being in that space. Now bring yourself back to your current reality, and celebrate the fact that nothing tragic has happened to you. Be grateful that you have lost nothing. Feel intense relief, as if it was all some sort of nightmare. Feel gratitude and thankfulness for each of those things. Celebrate the fact that the people that you love are still alive. This re-stimulates your gratitude for that person or thing and allows you to really feel gratitude. As you practice gratitude, you will find that little things can mean a lot, and that more and more great things will come to you. It is the best way to bring more into your life. Realize that tragic things happen to people all the time, but you were blessed enough to avoid them. Things could always be worse than they are. But they are not. That is a joy in itself.

Anytime you feel fear, irritation or anxiousness, one of the best ways to reverse this is to remember God's intense love for you. Simply remember Him and that He is there with you. He wants you to be happy and He wants to give you what you ask of Him. He loves to give you what you ask of Him and He most surely will. Remember that He would never bring you to a point in your life in order to hurt you. Remember that He is protecting you and guiding you to that which makes you happiest. Remember that you can trust in Him fully, and surrender everything to Him. Other ways to reverse a sour mood is to watch a stand up comedy video, or spend time with your pet or a loved one. Laughter is one of the best ways to attract happier circumstances in your future. Also try making a list of things that change your mood from negative to positive, and go down the list every time you are upset.

God has taught us that whatever we nurture grows, and that is how the law of attraction works. When we water a plant, it grows. When we feed our infants, they grow. That same concept applies to our spirit. If we nurture our spirit, then it will grow too. All we must do is become mindful of our thoughts, emotions, actions and words. Then we must nurture our happy thoughts and emotions, and create healthy, good energy. Because when you feel something deeply with intense emotion and passion, you attract more of that at an even faster rate. This is why it is very important to feel joy passionately. If you are feeling miserable about something, and you are feeling it passionately, then you are attracting more of that misery and you are attracting it quickly. But if you are feeling passionately joyous, then you are attracting all that makes you joyful very quickly. We always have a choice. We either nurture the negative energy within our spirits or nurture the positive energy and that is how we draw more into our lives. So nurture each great moment, and those moments will become more and more frequent.

I keep mentioning a faster frequency. This probably has you wondering, how long will it take to attract what I want? The answer is that there's no way of telling how long it will actually take. This means that you can attract something very fast, or you can attract something at a slower pace. It all depends on how much energy you are putting out. Which also means, that there is so much possibility that you can attract something within no time. The more energy you send out, the faster it arrives. What also might be of relief to you is that when using the law of attraction, there is no measure of size or magnitude when it comes to attracting what you want. You might perceive your pursuit as small or large. You are probably thinking a larger pursuit takes longer to attract. However, to the law of attraction size is irrelevant. What matters is energy. With strong energy, you can attract something that you might perceive as big in a speedy amount of time. You might feel like you have done all these techniques and your goals have still not manifested. You may even feel stuck and think, why hasn't it happened yet? A helpful technique in drawing things in at a faster rate (that has made a tremendous difference for myself when using the law of attraction) is adding a deadline to your goal. Choose your words carefully for your thoughts and be specific. Be as specific as possible. For example, if your goal is to have fifty million dollars by the time you are twenty-five, and you are currently twenty-four years old, you can use the following affirmation: "I am twenty-five years old and I have fifty million dollars." You can then add on more specifics to that statement, whatever else it is that you want in life, and repeat that affirmation daily. Adding a deadline, a time that you want to have the goals by, can really quicken the rate at which you draw things into your life.

You also need not worry about all the negative thoughts you have already had. No energy or thoughts manifest instantly. So if you have been thinking negative thoughts, you can turn your frequency around immediately with intense positive energy before anything troublesome can ever manifest.

One of the best ways to begin the manifestation process is to try and reach your subconscious mind. Our subconscious energy plays a very significant role in what manifests in our lives. Our subconscious mind is estimated to possess 88% of our mind's power, so it is very important to ground our life visions within our subconscious. Sometimes we are not feeling great and are not even aware of those suppressed negative emotions. However, once we become aware of our deepest emotions, we can turn that around and continue a positive frequency. This can be done through the use of meditation, gratitude, self-reflection, therapy, self-compassion and becoming present in order to remove that negative subconscious. The way to really figure out what is subconsciously bothering you is to become aware of your thoughts and your reactions to the people in your life. What triggers sadness or fear in you? Then go deeper. Why does it trigger sadness or fear in you? This also helps you clarify what you want and what you don't want. Once you have done this, then you can replace your unhealthy thoughts and subconscious with healthy affirmations and a healthy subconscious.

The best time to approach your subconscious is right before you go to sleep. This is when your subconscious is about to go to work, and when you are about to start dreaming. So, the fastest way to plant your visions into your subconscious is to **meditate, visualize, and speak your affirmations in your bed before you sleep and when you wake in the morning**. When you wake in the morning, you're still in the subconscious energy, and you begin your day with that energy so it is important to use these techniques both in the morning and at night before you sleep. Ever go to sleep upset or angry and wake up feeling more of the same? This is why it's important to feel good before you fall asleep. You're very likely to have another bad day if you go to sleep dwelling on your dissatisfaction with the previous day. As you lay in bed, feel joyous about having all the things you want in life, as if you already have them. Affirm to yourself out loud how you imagine your life to be, as if it already is. This is a great practice for improving a negative subconscious.

You may struggle with believing in the affirmations you tell yourself. Often times when we attempt to affirm something to ourselves it is natural to feel an inner resistance to those positive affirmations, because we feel like we are lying to ourselves. That struggle and resistance is also our subconscious. Usually what is bothering you subconsciously has something to do with a deficiency in the way you feel about yourself. The best way to deal with that deficiency is to force yourself to think of and write down memories in which you felt good about yourself.

Perhaps you received an award, perhaps you were praised for something, maybe you cooked something that everyone loved. Remember the times you did something great and you will reroute your thinking to a better direction. In doing so, you create a chain reaction in which you draw in more and more good thoughts about yourself. Good memories about yourself and your life are the best way to settle a resistive subconscious. Whenever something bothers you about yourself, remember an opposite memory in which you felt good about yourself. For example, if someone makes you feel stupid or unworthy, the way to reverse this would be to remember and write down all the times you did something or said something smart or praiseworthy. Say to yourself "I am smart," "I am worthy" and "I am more than enough."

And for the skeptics, what harm is there in feeling good? You can choose to feel happy or choose to feel sad. Why not try thinking happier thoughts instead of sulking around in the deep depression you have created?

Become present in the life you have desired and become still. In the stillness and wonderment of the world, that is where you will find the energy of miracles.

Celebrate when you are feeling good. Celebrate your current blessings and your future blessings. The more you feel celebratory, regardless of your current circumstances, the more you will have to celebrate about. With your celebration, you can deflect and dismiss the negativity of others. Their negativity will not mean anything to you when you are on a spiritual high, and when you are in the mental and emotional state of having achieved all of your dreams.

If we can maintain positive thinking in a habitual manner and if we continue to deflect all negativity, we will no longer attract the negative energy of others or negative circumstances. Happiness is a process and like any other process in life, it takes practice, so you probably won't find yourself one hundred percent happy for life after reading this book, but you can learn some tools that will help make you happier and how to make happiness a habit and practice in your life; you can train your mind to think in a healthier way. In a short amount of time, you will find that your experience of your life is more positive and happier.

And know this: Your thoughts matter. Your energy matters and your energy can make a tremendous difference in your life and in the world. That's a happy thought on its own.

I hope this knowledge brings relief and joy to each reader, and that it is the answer to your problems, as it was for me.

It is time to rejoice, to live free, to become a perpetual winner. Dream big and expect the best. Go after your dreams and intend them with passion. You can have it all. And once you have accomplished your greatest achievement, you can begin to believe that all of your forthcoming endeavors are even more possible for you. Just remember that when the stakes are high, your faith has to be higher in order to achieve success.

With that said, here are a few positive thoughts to begin with:

Your blessings are on their way.

Success is on its way.

Wealth is on its way.

Freedom is on its way.

Love is on its way.

Be sure that it is all on its way. Or, even better, that it has already arrived.

***

A note to remember while reading these happy thoughts: if the thought is important to you, say the thought repeatedly and visualize it. To help with this, highlight and make a list of the thoughts that are most important to you and focus on those specific thoughts. Also try using pictures to help you visualize, or create a vision board with pictures of all of your deepest goals and desires.

As you read along, you might feel that some of these thoughts will be hard to believe in. They may feel like lies because they will not always be a part of your reality as you are reading them. But with focus and unfaltering faith, they will become more and more believable to you. You must keep in mind that each thought has different levels of believability for each individual. If you simply cannot believe in a happy thought and cannot believe that it is possible for you, start off by focusing on a happy thought that is believable for you and then you can move on to the level of believing in what you had perceived as unattainable. Or, start off with a gratitude journal and begin writing down all the things you are grateful for in your life. The most important thing to keep in mind in regards to believability is, the more you focus on that fantasy being your reality, the more believable it becomes.

Do not forget how important it is to read these thoughts as if they truly are your current reality. Remember, think, feel, act and speak as if these thoughts are real.

1

HAPPY THOUGHTS ON THE SELF

I WANTED TO start with the self because I feel that we cannot begin a journey to happiness without beginning with the self. We cannot be happy until we are happy with ourselves. As Pastor Joel Olsteen says: "You'll never rise any higher than the way you see yourself." It is very important that we think well of ourselves if we want to succeed or find purpose in life. Without a healthy vision of ourselves, we cannot accomplish much.

The significance of these positive affirmations on the self is merely in their simplicity. You might be surprised how the simplest of thoughts can hold so much power for you. These simple affirmations on the self can help you see yourself through a better lens. They can teach you how great you are, and how great you can be. By repeating these words each day, you can begin to believe in them more and more, and build up your self-love and self-worth. The more you believe in them, the more you will see them in yourself. When you say to yourself, "I am brilliant," remember all the brilliant things you have done in your life or anytime you were great at something. Envision yourself being brilliant at your greatest passion. Walk with your brilliance in mind, talk to yourself as if you were brilliant, write headlines about yourself accomplishing great things, and feel the joy in it. It is also very important that you speak these thoughts out loud in order to draw them in.

One example of a great happy thought on the self is #100: "I did it." Say it out loud with intense passion. It might be that you did anything, small or large, that you thought you could not do, did not want to do, or resisted doing. The overall point is that you accomplished something, and you felt good about it just by saying it out loud and by reminding yourself that you are capable.

However, you must be cautious of your own ego in this process. Try to become aware of your own value and worthiness, to build confidence in yourself, without allowing your ego to dominate your awareness. You must be able to think healthy thoughts about yourself without letting your ego take over. If you find you are discouraged and depressed when you fail at something, stop and realize that this is your ego at work. It is the perfect opportunity to witness your ego in action, and to become aware of it. It is the ego that is concerned about social status and what others think, not the soul. It is the ego that is concerned about how much you have or have not accomplished. It is the ego that cares about your current circumstances. It is the ego that has attachment to certain outcomes. Once you are aware of your ego, you can begin to release the pain and step out of your ego into the sacredness of the present moment and into the sacredness of the power of your mind and your energy. You will begin to be able to detach yourself from your ego and the circumstances created by your ego, and you will be able to immerse yourself in the present moment without attachment to the outcomes. You will be able to be content despite your circumstances. This is how you release yourself from your ego.

If you struggle with thinking well about yourself, one exercise that may help with this is to make a list of your best qualities and save it. Put it up on your refrigerator, bulletin board, or somewhere that you'll see it a lot. This will help you focus on what you love or like about yourself. It is also important to keep in mind that in order to discover more great qualities about yourself, you must begin by being grateful for the good/great qualities you recognize in yourself. Try to truly feel gratitude about yourself and become aware of who you are. Keep record of these qualities in a gratitude journal and begin your sentences with: "I am so grateful for my…" or, "Thanks be to God that I am…."

Also consider making a list of the qualities you dislike about yourself; once you've finished, crumple it up and throw it away. This is a great way to cleanse yourself of the negative thoughts you have about yourself. The physical act of throwing this list away is how you can also rid your entire energy system and mind of the negative contents on this list. Try not to do this more than once so that you don't create a focus about the negative thoughts you have about yourself.

The summed basic idea you will need to grasp in this chapter is, not to believe you are so great from an egotistical approach, but simply to think better of yourself. Begin by focusing on what you love about yourself and focus on your best qualities. What do you really like about yourself? Do not focus on what you think is wrong with you. As Jon Kabat-Zinn puts it: "Pour energy into what is right with you."

1. I am enough.
    a. We tend to feel as though we are less than each time we are criticized by someone in our lives, or when we are simply too critical of ourselves. This affirmation is great to use when you are trying to build your own self-esteem and confidence. Just as we must practice sports and hygiene, we must practice how to think well of ourselves, because without a positive self-image, we will never be able to become the person we've always wanted to be.
2. I am more than enough.
    a. Once you have been able to convince yourself that you are enough just as you are, you can begin to start thinking you are more than enough for anyone in your life. The more you start to see it, the more the people around you will see it. You don't need to try and become what others want you to be. Teach people how to love and accept you for your own innate greatness by believing in it; that is authentic love. If you attempt to live your life in order to

please someone else, you will find yourself spiritually depleted. This is because critical people tend to continue to criticize no matter how much you have changed for them, simply because they have not yet learned how to appreciate life. "If you live by the approval of others, you will die by their rejection." ~Pastor Rick Warren.

3. I am well.
    a. To say this and to have the ability to truly believe it can be one of the greatest gifts in life. The best way to allow yourself to mean it would be to think of all the areas in your life in which you really are doing well. For example, you have the ability to breath, to walk or to see. If you are in good health, you are well, and that is a wonderful miracle in itself. If your heart, lungs, liver or stomach are functioning as they should be, say 'I am well.'
4. I am open to receiving.
    a. We tend to unconsciously deflect our ability to receive blessings by maintaining negative thinking. However, with a simple shift in our awareness we can become more

open. When we are spiritually open to the universe, we create a vacuum space for receiving. This affirmation is important because when you say it, you give off the energy of flexibility, and openness, which is a positive energy of trust. And when you emit the energy of trust—trusting God and the universe—you are positioning yourself as open and you become most available to receive blessings through your energy frequency.

5. I am free.
   a. Often times, in our own state of unconsciousness, stress and fear tend to make us feel trapped or stuck within our circumstances. We forget that through a simple change in our awareness, we can remember all the ways in which we are free in our lives. Use this affirmation to remind yourself how really free you are. Do you have the freedom to eat what you like? Do you have the ability to spend even some of your time as you like? Appreciate that, so that your freedom will continue to expand

in your life, to the point where it becomes absolute freedom.

6. I am important.

   a. At times in your life someone may have made you feel as though you were not important and disregarded you. It is up to you to remind yourself how important you are. Others will begin to see it. Remember what the people in your life will lack without you and remember why you are so important.

7. I am playing an important part in the big picture of life.

   a. Despite how some may have made you feel, you are being of service in the bigger picture of life. You already have and will continue to make a difference in someone's life. It may be that you have influenced someone in a conversation or have inspired them without knowing. Or your help may have changed someone's life. If you can continue to understand that God brings us into each person's life for a reason, you will never feel like your life is purposeless or that you have wasted any time here.

8. I am lovable.
    a. If someone has ever made you feel as though you are hard to love, or are not worthy of love, use this affirmation to remind yourself that you are easy to love. Think of all the qualities you possess that make you easy to love and write them down in a list.
9. I am brilliant.
    a. Think of a time in which you did or said something brilliant. Remember how good it made you feel, and say 'I am brilliant.' This way, you will create a positive train of thought and remember several other times in which you acted brilliantly. You will also think of more brilliant ideas.
10. I am talented.
    a. Think of all of your talents, small or large. Write them down and collect them on a piece of paper. Remember how talented you are and say it out loud. Feel gratitude for your talents and feel them expanding.
11. I am intelligent.
12. I am a genius.

a. Think of a time in which you did or said something that made you feel like you were a genius. Perhaps people around you praised you or called you a genius. Then say this affirmation aloud.
13. I am smart.
   a. Think of a time in which you did or said something that made you feel smart. Perhaps people around you were impressed with what you said. Then say: 'I am smart,' and get a positive train of thought going about yourself.
14. I am clever.
15. I am amazing.
16. I am kind.
   a. It is important that we think of ourselves as kind, because the energy of love is the most powerful energy we create. It is also important to be kind, authentically and intentionally, in order to draw more kindness into our lives and create good karma for ourselves. You must truly feel the beauty of kindness, embrace it and enjoy it.
17. I am generous.

a. It is important that we not only think of ourselves as generous, but that we take generous action as well in life. If we are authentically and intentionally generous, we will attract more generosity into our lives and create great karma for ourselves.
18. I am ambitious.
19. I am determined.
20. I am caring.
21. I am thoughtful.
   a. If anyone has ever made you feel as though you were unkind, or defined you as a mean person, simply state this affirmation to yourself. Remind yourself of how thoughtful you have been in your life, and bring to the forefront of your memory the times you did thoughtful things for others. This way you are creating your own positive definition of yourself.
22. I am funny.
   a. If anyone has ever made you feel as though you weren't funny—has told you that you are not funny or does not laugh at your jokes, use this affirmation to remind

yourself that you are funny. Think of all the times you made someone or a group of people laugh.

23. I am friendly.
    a. If you tend to think of yourself as unfriendly, or someone may have called you that in the past, and you would like to change that, begin using this affirmation to redefine yourself. You will start to see yourself as more and more friendly the more you use it.

24. I am joyful.
    a. If you constantly think of yourself as unhappy, use this affirmation to make yourself feel more joyful. Make a list of some of the blessings in your life in order to help shift your mood. The word joy also has a certain powerful charge behind it, since words carry energy behind them, so be aware of the power of the word joy.

25. I am incredible.
    a. To be incredible means to be so extraordinary that it's hard to believe. Albert Einstein, Steve Jobs and Oprah Winfrey all did incredible things in their

lives; hence they are defined as incredible. What they all had in common was one thing: they believed in themselves and they followed their passions. So begin to imagine yourself as an 'incredible' person and how that would look for you.

26. I am adventurous.

    a. You may not typically consider yourself adventurous and you may start feeling like you want to change that. Say this affirmation and envision yourself doing all sorts of adventurous things you want to try. Also, try remembering any adventurous things you have done in the past.

27. I am spontaneous.

28. I am optimistic.

    a. Many people consider themselves pessimists, and want to change that. If you use this affirmation and start to view yourself as an optimist you will begin to feel lighter in your being and begin to see all the possibilities your future holds. You will become more open to the good that life can have in store for you. Think of all the times you have been optimistic in the past and remind yourself of the optimism in you.

29. I am positive.
    a. To be positive can have multiple meanings, all still coinciding with thinking better of ones' self. This affirmation can not only help you feel more confident and certain about the decisions you make, but it can also help you feel like you are moving forward with great direction in your life.

30. I am honest.
    a. If anyone has ever called you a liar or made you out to be one, deflect their words and embrace this affirmation. Repeat it to yourself and really absorb the energy of this affirmation until you feel it. Do not allow someone else's negative opinion of you enter your thoughts and do not be consumed by their titles for you. You are always what you think are.

31. I am trustworthy.
    a. Think of all the people who would trust you without hesitating and all the times you have proven yourself to be trustworthy.

32. I am peaceful.
33. I am genuine.
34. I am creative.
    a. You have the ability to not only create your reality but to create your dreams and successes as well. It is important to think of yourself as creative in order to do that.
35. I am an inventor.
36. I am original.
37. I am inspiring.
38. I am brave.
    a. It is often times quite difficult for us to convince ourselves that we are brave when we are facing our greatest fears. This affirmation can help. Remind yourself of all the times you acted bravely and faced a fear. Take several deep breaths and feel the braveness you felt in those moments. Visualize yourself conquering your greatest fears.
39. I am courageous.
40. I am daring.
41. I am witty.
    a. Remember all the moments in which you

were witty and feel how good it felt. This thought is useful if you want to improve your social and networking skills.

42. I am insightful.
43. I am charming.
44. I am grateful.
45. I am successful.
    a. Visualize yourself in the success you want to be in. How do you want your success to look?
46. I am energetic.
47. I am dynamic.
48. I am compassionate.
49. I am loyal.
50. I am loving.
51. I am unique.
52. I am passionate.
53. I am imaginative.
54. I am confident.
    a. It can be hard to convince ourselves of our own confidence but this affirmation can help. The more you repeat it to yourself, the easier it will be to believe it. See yourself in circumstances in which you are confident in your actions.

55. I am strong.
56. I am independent.
57. I am extraordinary.
58. I am eternal.
59. I am precious.
60. I am beautiful.
61. I am gorgeous.
62. I am attractive.
63. I am young.
64. I am healthy.

   a. Many of us tend to believe that we are physically sick and hold on to the belief that we are sick after the trauma of having been diagnosed with an illness. Usually this means that we are more spiritually unwell, because our physical bodies are reflections of our spiritual health. In other words, our outer health is reflective of our inner health. If your health is not at its best, use this affirmation to help improve it. Visualize your body and your organs functioning properly and looking well. See yourself being in complete health and repeat this affirmation over and over. Also practice gratitude for all the healthy and functioning parts of your body. The bottom line? Changing the way you think can improve your health.

65. I am active.
66. I am driven.
67. I am powerful.
68. I am valuable.
69. I am worthy.
    a. We often unconsciously think we are unworthy of many things and it is our job to remind ourselves that we are always worthy. We are all worthy of the best things in life and deserve all of life's joys.
70. I am valued.
71. My opinions are valued.
    a. If someone you know makes you feel small when you speak, use this affirmation to visualize people asking your opinion and valuing what you say and repeat it to yourself. Focus on that rather than the negative attributes others try to create for you and you will create more experiences in which people value what you say.
72. I am loved.

73. I am cherished.
    a. At times someone in your life may make you feel small, so it is important to remember this affirmation and remind yourself of all the people who truly do cherish you. Think of all the good things about yourself and why people cherish you.
74. I am adored.
75. I am admired.
76. I am understood.
    a. When we have difficulties in our relationships, or are simply at odds with others, we tend to feel misunderstood. But there are many more things that our loved ones accept and understand about us than there are misunderstandings, and it is healthy in our thought process to remind ourselves that we are understood and most importantly, we are heard. Think of all the times someone really understood and heard you.
77. I am remembered.
    a. Use this if you find that the people in your life tend to forget about you.

78. I have an attractive physique.
79. I have a great personality.
80. I am respected.
    a. If you have been feeling unimportant, use this affirmation to visualize people respecting you and your opinion.
81. I have a respectable personality.
82. I have a likeable personality.
83. I have a sociable personality.
84. I am confident in my skills and capabilities.
85. I am a magnet of success and achievement.
86. I am a surplus of bliss.
87. I am healed.
    a. If you have not been doing well physically or spiritually use this affirmation to attract wellness.
88. I am safe.
    a. When you find yourself feeling afraid of possible outcomes or situations, use this affirmation to remind yourself that you are eternally safe. Visualize a constant bubble of protection that surrounds you in order to help you feel safer. As long as you believe you are truly safe and that God is keeping you safe, you will remain safe throughout

your life.

89. I am calm and collected.
90. I am happy.
    a. What must happen in your life for you to be truly happy? See it in your mind and be happy without it. Because chances are, even if you had it now, you probably would not be as happy as you think you'd be simply because you haven't yet learned how to be happy in the present moment. Remember, if we see it and feel it in our minds it has the same effect on us whether it has manifested or not. You can feel as though you have it *now*. Ultimately however, we can choose to be happy and grateful with our lives as they are now. In doing so, we will attract more happiness into our lives.
91. I am a fantastic cook.
92. I have great posture.
93. I have great public speaking skills.
94. I am capable of many things.
95. I know what to do.
    a. We often find ourselves in situations where

we are out of our comfort zone and tell ourselves "I don't know what to do." However, if we affirm to ourselves that we do know what to do, we will attract knowing what to do instead. When in doubt, remember this quote by Paul Williams and Tracey Jackson: "I don't know how to do this, but something in me does." Trust that you will figure out and know what to do.

96. I know what to say.
97. I always find the answer.
98. I always find a way.
99. I always find opportunities for success and take complete advantage of them.
100. I did it. I made it.
101. I have left my mark in the world.
102. My blessings arrive easy and smooth.
103. I always find ways to improve my life.
104. My inner peace is invincible.
105. There are so many things about me that are special.
    a. I am special because

    _____

    _____

106. There is no one like me.
107. I love me.
   a. We have to learn to truly love ourselves if we want to bring more love and happiness into our lives. It is important to practice this affirmation if you find you do not like yourself. As you continue to say it, it will become more believable for you and you will remember what there is to love about you.
108. I spread my light to all whom I encounter.
109. My art is brilliant.
110. My creations are phenomenal.
111. My creativity comes to me effortlessly.
112. I have accomplished each and every single thing that I have set out to accomplish.
113. I have accomplished tremendous prestige through the passions of my life.
114. I have made a difference in the world.
115. I articulate my thoughts well.
   a. People who are afraid of public speaking will find this affirmation useful. Use it when you have a public speaking event coming up soon.

116. I am naturally clever during conversations.
117. I am an infinite winner.
118. I shine in my life.
119. My health is invincible.
120. I have the strongest immune system imaginable.
    a. This affirmation is great for those who often think they are going to get sick and therefore attract it. When you tell yourself that your immune system is invincible, you create that and find yourself in a state of constant well-being and health.
121. I have so much energy.
    a. This affirmation is great if you think of yourself as a lazy person. Begin telling yourself that you have more energy and you will start to feel it.
122. I am capable of achieving success.
123. I believe that I am going to achieve success.
124. I trust that I am being lead to something that is great for me.
125. I trust the path that I am on.
126. People are kind to me.
127. People receive me well.
    a. If you are someone who is afraid of being rejected by a person or a group of people,

this is a great affirmation to use in order to help you have more confidence in yourself and to learn not to be afraid of people. Again, the more you say it and think it, the more you will believe it. Always expect that people will receive you well. If you carry positive energy with you when you enter a room, you will most often find your experiences with others pleasant.

128. I live in the present joy.
   a. Use this affirmation to find the joy in the now, to find what brings you joy now and what you have to be grateful for now.
129. Wherever I go, I attract good things.
130. I will attract the way.
   a. Know that if you can successfully put your desired vision of your life into your subconscious, you will attract the way to accomplishing your vision. The best way to ground something into your subconscious is to visualize or meditate on it before you sleep and when you wake in the morning. The fastest way to reach your subconscious is in the morning and at night because

those times are nearest to the times that we sleep, and our subconscious goes to work while we sleep. Visualize as often as you can for a stronger, faster energy frequency. In addition, you must feel intensely joyous and act as though your desired reality is your current reality. The universe will arrange itself to your favor and guide you to your desires. You will attract the next steps and actions you need to take.

131. Tomorrow, I'll do better.
132. My positive energy makes a tremendous difference in the world.
133. My positive energy makes a tremendous difference in my life.
134. The peace and contentment of being when you are on the path of your great destiny.
135. The feeling of wholeness when you finally realize what you were meant to do.
136. I am living as the best version of myself possible.
137. I start with good, and I end up with the best.
    a. This affirmation is great to use in order to attract the best things in life. When you are grateful with simply the good things in life, you will find yourself attracting the best

things in life as well.

138. My possibilities are infinite.

139. I am completely satisfied and happy with…

    a. _____

    _____

140. I'm happy and today is going to be a great day.

    a. Say this one every morning when you look in the mirror. Speak it into existence.

141. I am so satisfied.

    a. When you say this out loud, slowly and intentionally, it really creates a catalyst chain of positive thoughts for you.

142. I am so satisfied with…

    a. What are you satisfied with today and right now? Make a list of as many things as you can think of that you are a satisfied with and I can guarantee that it will put you on a frequency of satisfaction. If you hold on to this frequency for as long as you can, you will draw in the things that you are seeking. You've got to stay in the energy of satisfaction in order to get where you want to go. Esther Hicks says: "The reason that you want every single thing that you want is because you think you will feel really good when you get there. But if you don't feel really good on your way to there, you can't get there. You have to be satisfied with that is, while you're reaching for more.

What are some of your own, personal happy thoughts for yourself?

___

___

___

___

___

___

___

___

___

___

A Thousand and One Happy Thoughts

2

RANDOM HAPPY THOUGHTS

ON LIFE

THIS IS WHERE it gets fun. These thoughts are meant to be exciting and uplifting. They are general happy thoughts that everyone can enjoy. Many of them will help you imagine having great life experiences. The thought of walking into your very first, brand new dream home can be thrilling for anyone. Envision your dream home exactly the way you would like it to be: the design, the architecture, your furniture, your dream back yard. When you're in your car driving home from work, act as if you were just given the news about getting your dream home, or whatever it is that you are pursuing, and start screaming in celebration. Pretend that you never have to go back to the job you hate. Laugh, shout, feel the excitement! Buy yourself something to celebrate. You need to act, speak, feel and think in accordance with these thoughts of excitement and joy. In addition to this, we cannot attract a brand new beautiful home or great life experiences without first being grateful for the space we live in or the great moments we've already experienced in life. You must first have gratitude in order to manifest your dream home or the best experiences your life has to offer.

In this chapter, you will find almost every thought you will need in order to draw in more exciting and joyful things into your life. Again, it is also important to use some of these thoughts to practice gratitude for the things about your life that you are already happy with. This way, you will continue to attract more great circumstances into your life and you will also be able to keep the blessings you have already acquired by remaining conscious of them and grateful for them.

Try your best to truly let each thought resonate within you and "feel the joy rising" from them as though they are your current reality. Doing so before you go to sleep and when you wake in the morning will help ground these thoughts into your subconscious. That is how you will attract them.

143. My energy matters.
144. I have arrived. I have found my way.
145. I am home.
    a. What does home look like for you and what do you want the context of your home life to be?
146. We did it. We made it.
147. I am set for life. We are set for life.
148. I am so excited for all the great things to come.
149. I am taken care of.
150. I am taking care of myself.
151. I am beyond blessed in my life.
152. Blessings surprise me often, everywhere I go.
153. I am now living the life of my dreams.
    a. What does this look like for you? Visualize it and truly feel the joy of it.
154. Through each life experience, I am sure that only good will come.
155. I love everyone. (Feeling love for everyone around you.)
    a. It is important to feel love for everyone, to look for the best qualities in each person that is in your life, in order to stay on a

positive energy frequency. Try to love each person as much as you can or have compassion for people who are difficult to love. By focusing on the best things in people, not only will you bring out the best qualities in the people around you, but you will also draw more positive people into your life.

156. I have discovered my passion, and I am so grateful for that.

    a. This affirmation is great for those who find themselves unable to figure out what they want to do in their life and what their purpose is. By using this affirmation, you can draw in the answer. As Rumi says: "What you seek is seeking you." Open yourself up to receiving and allow the answer to come to you.

157. I am so happy and grateful that I have achieved absolute, everlasting success.

158. My pursuit is something minute compared to what I have already achieved.

159. I am grateful to have plenty of friends.

160. I am so happy to have friends who are there for me, friends who understand me, friends that I have

so much fun with and friends whom I love.
161. Great things have happened in my life.
   a. Try to remember every single wonderful thing that has happened in your life and write them down on a list. Frame it if you need it to serve as a reminder in your life. This is how you will attract more great things into your life.
162. Miraculous things have happened in my life; my life is miraculous.
163. Happiness comes to me effortlessly, in all possible ways.
164. Great opportunities always present themselves to me.
165. I am feeling one hundred percent satisfied.
166. I attract only people's love and admiration.
167. Miraculous news has arrived.
   a. What is the best possible news you could receive today? Imagine it arriving right now.
168. My life is good and great.
169. My life is spectacular.
170. I believe in good people.
   a. It is important to believe that there are

good people in this world in order to attract more good people into your life. Also try always to focus on the good in people.

171. I believe in trustworthy people.
172. I have great trust in people.
173. I thank God that I always have the freedom to do whatever I want, whenever I want to.
174. My life is exactly the way I want it to be.
175. More good and great things are coming my way.
176. Miraculous things are coming my way.
177. I am grateful to have attracted like-minded people into my life.
178. I am grateful to be surrounded by like-minded people who appreciate, love and support me.
179. I thank God for all peace, harmony and love in my life.
180. I am so grateful that I always get to do the things that make me happy.
    a. Teaching yourself this thought is a great way to set yourself up for success in the future. You will find yourself always doing the things that make you happy.
181. Everyone accepts me for who I am.
    a. Often times, we find that important people in our lives are not accepting of the way we

are and who we want to be and this affirmation can change that. By using this affirmation, you can make everyone in your life more and more accepting of who you are.

182. Everyone accepts the way I choose to live.

183. I live the life I imagined.

184. I stay inspired.

185. I believe that I have a bright prospect in the future.

186. Something great is going to happen very soon. I can feel it.

    a. Use this affirmation constantly as a reminder that your greatest dreams are very close. It will help keep you on a positive energy frequency. What is the best thing that could happen to you right now?

_____

_____

187. I always find myself enjoying sunny weather.

188. I have eternal free time.

    a. We all tend to think that we are busy and are constantly feeling a lack of time. This affirmation is a great way to attract more

> free time into your life and will allow you to feel like you have more time in your life.

189. I have more than enough time to do all the things I want to do in each of my days.
190. I am so grateful that I have the ability to walk and run.
    a. The sad truth is, not everyone in the world is able to say they have legs. That's why it is important to use this affirmation, whether it is true for you or not, in order to attract the best possible version of legs you can have.
191. I thank God that I have the ability to see (all the beautiful things in the world).
192. I thank God for my nose.
193. I thank God for the ability to smell the alluring aromas of the world.
194. I am so grateful for my excellent health.
    a. It important to truly feel gratitude for our health in order stay healthy throughout our lives.
195. I thank God for my skin.
196. I thank God for my face.
197. I thank God for my teeth.
198. I thank God for the ability to smile.

199. I thank God for the ability to show expression through my face.
200. I thank God for my ears.
201. I thank God for the ability to hear all the beautiful sounds and voices in the world.
202. I thank God for my hands and all that I can do with them.
203. I thank God for every finger I have, and all that I can feel with them.
204. I thank God for every toe that I have.
205. I am grateful for my rear end, and the soft comfort of sitting on it.
206. I am grateful for my arms that allow me to reach out and receive.
207. I am grateful for my feet that take me everywhere I want to go.
208. I am grateful for my plump chest.
209. I am grateful for the slimness of my waist.
210. I am grateful for all the beautiful curves of my body.
211. I am so grateful for my bedroom.
212. I am so grateful for the space that I am blessed with.
213. I am as happy as I possibly can be.

214. I am so grateful and happy that I own my own home, the house of my dreams; I am so happy and grateful for the home that I am blessed with.
    a. What does your dream home look like? See it in your mind and draw your own blueprint of it.

    _____

    _____

215. I am so grateful for my incredibly warm, soft, comfortable, cozy bed for when it's chilly outside and I am tired.
    a. Visualize yourself waking up in your bed, wrapped tightly in your warm blankets, your bedroom window is open, the spring breeze is coming through, and you can hear the birds chirping, and see the brightness of the sun coming in, the trees, the sky, the green grass. You breathe deeply and freely; you are calm; your chest is light, and you feel grateful.
216. I have conquered life.
217. I have constant and eternal stability in my life.
218. Things are looking up for me.
219. Everything I ever need to accomplish my goals unfolds before my eyes.

220. I accomplish my goals quickly.

221. I accomplished my goal in _____ day(s).

222. I accomplished my goal in _____ month(s).

223. I accomplished my goal in _____ year(s).

224. I love giving. I feel great when I give.

    a. Giving and service are excellent examples of the law of karma or the golden rule. The best way to look at service is that not only are you doing good for others, but you are also creating great karma for yourself. This makes it easier for us to enjoy the act of service, especially when we are not feeling appreciated. It is important to remember that we do not need appreciation when we serve and that we will receive blessings tenfold when we feel good about doing good for others. That is key. The world is here to serve you as you are here to serve it.

225. I am so grateful to have more than enough to give.

226. I am free forever, in every way possible. I have eternal, everlasting freedom. I am so happy and grateful to have absolute freedom.

227. I live free.

228. I thank God for all of this freedom.
229. These moments are mine.
230. I feel great.
231. I feel elated.
232. I laugh often.
233. I am so grateful for how beautiful my life is.
    a. Visualize your life being beautiful, in however way you choose to define a beautiful life.
234. I am so happy and grateful that I get to do all the fun things there is to do in the world.
235. I thank God that I am both physically and spiritually well.
236. I am so grateful for the hot, soothing showers that I get to enjoy each morning as the sunlight peaks through my bathroom window.
237. I thank God that I am able to live independently.
238. I thank God that I get to be completely in charge of my life.
239. I thank God that I get to live eternally free within my own space. I am so happy and grateful that I get to enjoy constant and everlasting personal space.
240. I am so happy and grateful that I always have constant and perpetual "me-time."

241. That liberating, joyful satisfaction of getting to enjoy free time once you get home from work.
242. I am grateful for the comfort and joy of relaxation.
243. I am so happy and grateful to have the things I want and to continuously receive more of the things I want. I always visualize having everything I want, and then I receive it.
244. I am at peace and overjoyed with my life.
245. I thank God that I can do whatever I please with my time each day. I am so grateful that all of my time is eternally mine and for doing the things that I love to do.
246. I am so happy and grateful that I weigh the weight I want to way.
247. I am so happy and grateful that I weigh _____ pounds.
    a. What would be your ideal weight? Writing a specific number down and having a vision of it will help you draw it in.
248. I am so happy and grateful that I have the physique of my dreams.
249. I am so happy and grateful that I have vibrant, clear skin that stays clear.
250. I am so happy and grateful that I have smooth,

defined skin.

251. I am so happy and grateful that I have the car of my dreams. I love my brand new car.
    a. Luxurious with leather seats, a rear view camera and a fancy, high-tech dashboard. What is the car of your dreams?

    _____

252. I am so happy and grateful that I have the job of my dreams.
    a. What is the job of your dreams?

    _____

253. I love my job.
254. I love doing my job.
255. I love the environment of my job.
256. My workplace is beautiful.
257. I like my coworkers.
    a. This is a great affirmation to use if you don't have a great relationship with your current coworkers. You will either form a better relationship with them or attract co-workers you like into your workplace.
258. I am grateful that my coworkers are supportive and kind.
259. I am grateful that my boss appreciates my work.
    a. This affirmation is great if you have a boss

who constantly complains about you. Your relationship with your boss will either change, you will be distanced from them somehow, or you will find yourself dealing with a new boss who appreciates you.

260. I am grateful to have a job in which I get to choose my own work schedule. I am so grateful that I get to work when I please.

261. I thank God that I am able to work from home successfully.

    a. What would this look like for you?

262. The moment you truly feel your own freedom. The glory of that first breath of free air.

    a. What would have to happen to make you feel free? Imagine that it happened right now.

_____

_____

263. Spontaneously going swimming on a hot summer night, in your amazing pool with loved ones, enjoying the cool water, making jokes, laughing together in carefree spirits.

264. Enjoying delicious meals at home with loved ones and then having your favorite dessert. Cheesecake,

Hershey's sundae pie, chocolate chip cookies, brownies or pazookies. What is your favorite dessert?

265. The simple pleasure of riding your bike and observing all that you pass.
266. Going to dinner with your loved ones, at one of your favorite restaurants, eating one of your favorite meals.
267. The accomplished feeling of receiving your diploma.
268. The beauty of falling asleep in a flower field.
269. Having several bouquets and flower arrangements of your favorite flowers set up beautiful throughout your home. What are your favorite flowers? Tulips, Roses, Baby's Breath, Peonies, Hydrangeas?
    a. What are your favorite flowers?

    _____

    _____

270. Remodeling your bedroom, bathroom, or your entire house to the exact designs you've been wanting.
    a. What would this look for you? What changes to your home décor have you been wanting to make?

271. Tiny, round little birds sitting on a branch outside your window, chirping in the sunlight.
272. The cool feeling of the wind when it hits your cheeks as you drive, the sun shining over the lush greenery that surrounds you.
273. The sound the wind makes when it blows outside of your window.
274. Sinking into the couch after a long day of completing tasks.
275. Finally receiving that good news you've been dying to hear.
    a. What would be the best possible news you can receive right now?

276. That cool, relaxed, clean feeling after an evening shower.
277. Building a fort in your house or yard with blankets and furniture, then sleeping in it as if you are a child again.
278. Slumber parties with your loved ones.
    a. A marathon of your favorite movies,

popcorn, candy, pizza, hot wings and foam mattresses with soft blankets and fluffy pillows.
279. Being absolutely hilarious and making all of your loved ones laugh.
280. Being alive.
281. Breathing.
   a. We tend to take for granted the joy of the ability to breath until we lose it. This affirmation teaches you how to appreciate this simple yet dire blessing.
282. Hugging a loved one.
   a. We must always appreciate the ability to hug our loved ones while they are still with us, so that we can continue to be blessed with their embraces.
283. Hiking up a mountain or through a forest and watching the sunset.
284. Going camping with your loved ones.
285. The warm joy of summer nights.
286. Sweatpants, a comfy sweater, a soft blanket, and a cup of sweet tea on a chilly winter night.
287. Waking up in the early morning in the comfort of your bed, as if the rest of the world is asleep. You are at peace with your life, content and still as the

sun rises.

288. Waking up to rainfall in the comfort of your bed and the joy of knowing you can stay in your fluffy comforter as long as you like.

289. Sending awesome text messages at night to a loved one and receiving them back.

290. Enjoying hot bubble baths in the evening, with candles and luxurious bubble bath soaps and scents.

291. Owning your very own large, luxurious bathtub with a large glass window that overlooks an amazing view.

292. Having soft hands.

293. Remembering that there's always tremendous hope, and that anything can happen.

294. An infinity pool that blends into lush green mountains and a wide, open sea.

295. Getting perfect manicures and pedicures with loved ones.

296. Cute coffee mugs.

297. Going bowling with loved ones.

298. Inspirational dancing.
    a. I always think of Beyonce. What type of dancing inspires you?

299. Gardening in your very own, grand garden, filled with all your favorite flowers, trees, fruits and vegetables.

    a. What would you keep in your garden?

300. The simple pleasure of enjoying the green of your own garden in the sunlight.
301. The freedom of knowing you get to stay home as long as you like, for the rest of your life.
302. Decorating your home with flower centerpieces that you made, using your favorite flowers from your own garden.
303. Stargazing on a soft blanket outside, under a moonlit sky filled with stars, absolutely as bright as imaginable.
304. The freedom of finally finishing college for good.
305. The incredible warmth and softness of a blanket that has just been taken out of the dryer, then wrapping it around your body and sitting on the couch.
306. Landing your dream job immediately after college.
307. The simple joy of coming home to a perfectly

clean home.

308. Enjoying the smell of your freshly cleaned pajamas after taking an evening bath.
309. Summer barbeques with your loved ones, in your dream back yard.
310. Dancing and laughing all night with the people you love.
311. Feeling happy with everyone around you.
312. That elevated feeling of swimming in vast aqua waters and lying on a Caribbean beach while the sun is setting.
313. Going to an amazing concert with loved ones.
314. Winning a tournament you've been preparing for.
315. Getting an A on a paper you worked very hard on.
316. The freedom and joy of knowing that you don't have to go to work the next morning.
317. Seeing results on the scale.
318. Having baby soft, smooth skin; The feeling of baby soft skin.
319. The joy of finding something you truly value after losing it.
    a. What have you lost that you've been dying to find? Imagine it showing up right now. You may attract it back into your life by

affirming it.

___

320. Getting to dress up in glamorous perfection for a formal event. Perfect hair, perfect makeup, perfect dress.
321. Watching your favorite show after work or school.
322. Winning a prize. Money, a car, a vacation, you name it.
323. Seeing a smile on someone's face after you've helped them.
324. A victorious ending to an epic story.
325. Laying in bed, visualizing perfect scenarios for your life.
326. Finding the perfect words.
327. Enjoying the dock of a lake with a loved one, carefree, dipping your feet, pondering, relaxing, and reading.
328. Big, cozy balconies with amazing views. Some of them your very own, attached to your dream home.
    a. What does your dream balcony look like?

    ___

    ___

329. Being almost there, and then getting there.
330. Colorfully bright balloons.
    a. I think of Disneyland balloons.

331. Enjoying amazing views.

332. Taking the perfect picture.

333. Smore bonfires in your backyard. Hersey's chocolate, marshmallows, Graham crackers and Recess Peanut Butter Cups.

334. Going to a gorgeous spa, getting a massage, facial, manicure and pedicure with your loved ones.

335. Girls day and night out.
   a. What would you do if you had one day and one evening to spend with your girlfriends?

   _____

   _____

336. Guys day and night out.
   a. What would you do if you had one day and one evening to spend with your friends?

   _____

   _____

337. Feeling passionate about something.

338. Feeling confident about a decision.

339. That peaceful and joyful feeling of being carefree.

340. Getting a new pet.
   a. What pet have you been wanting to get?

   _____

341. The excitement and joy of Disney movies on a cozy night, on your cozy couch with popcorn and candy.
    a. What are your favorite Disney movies?

    _____

    _____

342. The excitement of your favorite epic movies on a cozy night, on your couch with popcorn and candy.
    a. What is your favorite epic movie? Harry Potter, Lord of the Rings, Star Wars, you name it.

    _____

343. That satisfied feeling after watching an inspirational movie.
344. The feeling of relief and bliss after completing a big project, knowing that you'll never have to work on it again.
345. Enjoying your toilet on the morning of your first day off. That feeling of release and relief. And then taking a hot shower right after.
346. Your hot cup of coffee on your first day off.
347. My Mondays are great, because I spend them the way I love to.
348. A stunningly gorgeous man or woman.
349. The scent of cologne.

350. The scent of perfume.
351. A full head of silky hair.
352. Puppies.
353. Having your very own elaborate tree house in the woods where you slumber with your favorite people.
354. Remembering that you have the whole summer to do all the things you've been wanting to do.
    a. What do you want to do this summer?

    _____

    _____

355. Having the loyalty of a loved one.
356. Being reassured that someone truly values, loves and protects you.
357. The bliss of feeling safe and secure.
358. Enjoying the sparkle of city lights at night.
359. That satisfactory feeling after writing something great.
360. That amazing feeling of passion, enlightenment and motivation after being inspired.
361. That great feeling of accomplishment and liberation after finishing homework.
362. Watching Oprah and feeling whole.
363. Taking awesome pictures in photo booths.

364. When everything falls into place perfectly and smoothly.
365. Enjoying your reflection in the mirror.
366. Experiencing a red carpet event and being on the red carpet.
367. Being recognized and honored for your work.
368. The thrill of winning an award.
369. The joy of going to bed, knowing you can sleep as long as you want to.
370. Making it big and appearing on the Oprah Winfrey Network.
371. When a song is so inspiring and uplifting that it makes you dance.
372. The loyalty of a pet.
373. Lazy days.
374. Going to the warmth, comfort, and coziness of your bed after being out at night.
375. When the perfect song plays on your car radio and you soak in every second of it as you sing along.
376. Having an inspirational conversation with people you love and enjoy being around.
377. The comfort of belonging.
378. That satisfied, energized feeling of waking up in the morning after getting more than enough sleep.
379. That uplifting feeling when you remember

something hilarious that happened and are unable to control your laughter.

380. The cozy joy of Christmas Eve. Christmas lights, Christmas trees, Christmas music, matching Christmas pajamas, Christmas Day and Christmas presents.
381. Feeling one hundred percent confident in your faith.
382. Designing the perfect kitchen for your home.
    a. What would this look like for you?

    _____

    _____

383. Having your very own cozy movie theater in your home, designed by you, and enjoying movies in it with loved ones.
384. Having a window bed.
385. Having your very own grand, walk in closet, with shoe shelves, mirrors, lights and built in drawers.
386. Having your very own King size bed.
387. Having your very own clean, organized office, fully furnished and designed by you, and everything is in the place you'd like it to be.
388. Having your very own dream swimming pool with a luxurious jet Jacuzzi.

389. Having your own basketball court.
390. Owning acres of green land, each acre all yours, with flower fields, tree groves, orchards, and gardens.
391. Having a stockpile of your favorite shampoo and conditioner.
392. Waking up to a cozy December snowfall and watching TV in bed.
393. Remembering that it's never too late to start again.
394. The simple pleasure of swimming in a clean pool, on a hot summer's day.
395. Summer pool parties in your dream back yard with all your loved ones. Barbeque, fruit drinks and floaties.
396. The tremendous release and lightness of forgiveness.
397. Writing down all the good things that have happened to you this year on little pieces of paper, putting them in a jar and collecting them throughout the year, then emptying the jar and reading them at the start of the New Year.
398. Enjoying a hilarious movie with loved ones. With pizza and garlic sauce, popcorn and candy, hot wings and soda.
399. Laughing your hardest at silly things with loved

ones until you tear up and your stomach hurts.

400. Lying in the soft grass, arms outstretched, your back is flat against the earth in comfort. You are looking up in amazement at the open blue sky and the woolly white clouds.

401. Enjoying a picnic with loved ones. Delicious foods in a basket at your side: mangos, strawberries, grapes, turkey sandwiches and popcorn.

   a. What would you bring to your picnic?

   _____

   _____

402. The joy of singing in the morning.

   a. Gretchen Ruben, author of The Happiness Project, recommends singing in the morning because it shifts your energy frequency to an uplifting one. Try it while taking a shower or while you're making breakfast.

403. Oversized warm sweaters in the wintertime.

404. Various colored kittens in one room. Soft, fluffy, playful and purring.

405. Walking into your favorite retail store and being told that the entire store now belongs to you, and that everything is in your size.

406. Staying up late with your siblings and goofing around.
407. Spontaneous dessert outings.
408. The thrill of opening your emails and all the exciting news they bring you.
409. Basketball games with your friends or family.

What are some of your own random happy thoughts for your life?

3

HAPPY THOUGHTS ON GOD

THIS CHAPTER'S PURPOSE is to show readers how to think well of God. Often times, we think negatively of God without realizing it. When we doubt that our blessings will arrive, we also doubt God's generosity and capabilities. These little doubts are always what sever our chances in accomplishing our dreams. You must not hesitate in your belief in God's Grace. You must not doubt it. When your energy or faith is hesitant, your desires will not manifest. But when you are convinced that your blessings will arrive, you will draw them in, because you were certain in God's Grace. Always think to yourself: "why should God bless me if I doubt that He will?" God is more generous than we think.

You also cannot worry about how to manifest your desires. God wants you to leave that to Him. He wants you to trust Him with "the how." That is why he only asks us to pray and have faith, not to figure out how. He wants us to follow His guidance along our journey. Through our own stillness and trust, we can find the answers He provides us with. Both the Quran and The Bible, along with almost every world religion, encourage us to trust in God when we simply do not know what to do next. The Quranic verse 3:159 states: "Put your trust in God. God loves those that trust (in Him)." And in The Bible, Matthew 21:12 states: "If you have faith when you pray, you will be given whatever you ask for." There is a reason that all the wisdoms and traditions of the world teach us the importance of trusting God. We simply cannot be guided to the answers, next steps, or blessings without it. All we have to do is ask, trust with absolute certainty, and be open to receiving.

Thank Him each day for your current blessings, and for your future blessings. Be so certain in their arrival that you thank Him ahead of time. That is how they will show up in your life. That is how to show God that you truly trust in Him. Know that His blessings are on their way.

Hamad

In the Quran, verse 14:7, God states: "If you are grateful, I will surely give you more and more." Here, God encourages us to practice gratitude because it places us on a positive energy frequency and provides us with more blessings. God asks us to be grateful for own benefit and well-being—not because He is in need of our gratitude. God is The One exception to the gratitude rule; He remains in our lives whether we are grateful for Him or not.

When you find yourself feeling discouraged or disheartened, remember God's unconditional love for you. Remember that He is rooting for you, that He loves you and loves to bless you. Carry these thoughts with you, wherever you go. He wants you to be happy. Feel His love, and remember that He is preparing the best for you. If you simply trust that the life you desire will come to pass, you will see that trusting God and life has always been the answer.

So ask God for your desires, but with celebration that they have already arrived. And be sure that God is always guiding us to the best possible outcome.

410. I love God.

411. I am being of service to God; God is using me for a purpose.

    a. It feels wonderful for us to know and remember this affirmation. Use it even when you are not sure what purpose you are serving. You will know soon.

412. I trust and know that God will provide for me.

413. God is always guiding me to the best possible outcome.

414. God is love.

415. I am deserving of His blessings, because He created me.

    a. We tend to subconsciously think that we will never be blessed with great things in life because we have done so much wrong to ourselves and to others in life. However, the best way to right our wrongs is to start thinking well of God and to understand that God is beyond human grudges and sees passed your past. He would not have created you if He did not believe you to be deserving of His blessings, but He will only bless you if you truly believe in His Mercy.

416. I know that God loves me. His love for me is unconditional.

417. I know that God loves to bless me.

418. I know that God wants me to be happy.

419. God is The Most Generous and loves to give.

420. God gave me true value and I am always conscious of it.

421. God will bless me with what I have asked Him for because He is capable of all things great and miraculous.

422. I know my heart will never misguide me because my heart was created by God Himself.

423. God has a great plan for my life and He will guide me to it.

424. God is the Most Gracious.

425. God is gentle and compassionate.

426. My blessings from God are on their way.

427. God always blesses me with better than what I asked Him for.

428. God has blessed me with all of the things that I desire.

429. God is persistent in granting me the things I love and I am persistent in doing for God the things that

He loves.

430. God made it happen.
431. When I believe that God will bless me, He always makes a way.
432. God is always protecting me.
    a. If you find yourself fearing certain situations, picture yourself with a protection bubble around you that is from God and that this protection bubble is impenetrable. This can help reassure you that you are safe.
433. God loves to forgive and has forgiven me. God loves forgiveness.
434. God loves passion.
435. God is The Most Merciful.
436. God always guides me to what is best for me.
437. God has blessed me with great people and great circumstances because I knew He would.
438. God will make it better; God will make all of my affairs better and better.
439. When I whisper out to God, He comes to me at speed.

Hamad

What are some of your own, personal happy thoughts on God?

4

HAPPY THOUGHTS ON FAMILY

THIS CHAPTER IS meant to help you think well of your family and the circumstances regarding your family. It can help you better your severed relationships with certain family members and help create an energy of love for your family. It will also help eliminate your dysfunctional thoughts about your family members as well as any wrong assumptions that you may have made about a family member. Some of these thoughts may already be true about your relationship with your family members, and some you might wish to be true for you and your family members. Regardless, thinking them will either better your relationships with your family members or help you maintain healthy and great relationships with your family members. If you are in need of making amends with family, or would simply like to continue great ties with your family, this is the chapter for you.

Remember, you cannot create great relationships with your family members without first being grateful for the relationships you already have with them. Do your best to focus on what is right about your relationships, and what you like/love about your family members in order to draw more of that into your life. You will discover new positive things about your relationships or simply notice a change in behavior from your family members.

It is also important to, as the Japanese proverb puts it, "be like a bamboo" when it comes to important relationships in your life. The more flexible you are and the less you resist about these relationships, the less circumstances you will need to resist. In other words, if you do not inwardly resist these relationships or resist the circumstances they bring, they will not persist. If you do not fear them or focus on and feel the negativity they bring you or cause you, they will not continue to show up in your life. If there is someone in your family that has a difficult personality or creates a lot of negative circumstances in your life it is important to have perspective and a higher awareness in order to eliminate the negativity they bring to your life. We often find ourselves wondering how to deal with their negativity. Do we remove them from our lives or distance ourselves from them?

It is usually ideal to create distance between ourselves and our family members that seem to create conflict with us and with others, however that is not always the only solution or means of finding peace. First, I recommend praying for their happiness. They are almost always behaving negatively because they are spiritually unwell and need healing, so pray for them. Pray for their health and well-being. Not only does this create happy energy for them, but it also creates excellent karma for you and makes way for more blessings within *your* life. It also creates happier, more peaceful circumstances for your future. If the family member that is creating conflict and negativity in the lives of their loved ones becomes a happy, spiritually balanced person, they will no longer create this conflict and negativity.

Second, make your focus regarding them and your relationships about peace, freedom and love. Become grateful for any kind of peace, freedom and love in your life and the relationships of this sort that you already have with others. Also be grateful for any moments of peace, tranquility and freedom you find in your life now so that you may create more of that. You will either be drawn away from them, or you will see a positive change in their behavior.

If you find that this family member is attempting to pull you into conflict, it is important never react to their anger or emotional outbursts. This is a cry for help or attention and also a way to invite others into their own inner struggles so that they do not feel so alone. We tend to subconsciously want others to suffer with us, therefore we accuse or blame or get angry with those around us. So, when someone is inviting you into their personal pain, it is important to be flexible. If they accuse you of something or are simply unkind to you, do not reciprocate their bad behavior. If you want to end the cycle of bad karma, be as kind as you can and have as much understanding as you can. Try to create a healthy distance between you and them without completely cutting ties. The Japanese proverb goes on to say: "Be like a bamboo; it bends but does not break; it is flexible, yet firmly rooted. The bamboo that bends is stronger than the oak that resists." In today's world being flexible is seen as being passive, however, it is truly nothing of the sort. It is wise to be flexible, as well as strong (like the bamboo), because when you are flexible and forgiving, you draw only positive circumstances into your life. It is the healthier reaction and approach for not only their future, but also, for your own. You allow for the circumstances to get better without having to exhaust yourself with the energy of fighting or resistance. It can be much more difficult to resist the ego and to stay centered. This is why *the bamboo that bends is stronger than the oak that resists.*

440. I am so happy and grateful that my family and I get to live near each other; I am so happy and grateful that my family and I are always close to each other.
441. I am so happy and grateful for the fun times I get to share with my family.
    a. What fun things do you love doing with your family? It might be celebrating Thanksgiving, going shopping, or going to dinner.

    _____

    _____

442. I thank God that my family members are alive and that I can spend time with them.
443. I am so grateful for my child's/children's strong health.
444. I thank God for my family's good health.
    a. Your mother, father, sister, brother, children and so on. Is there someone in your family who is struggling with their health? This is a great affirmation to use in order to attract good health for them.
445. I love my family.
446. Going on grand vacations with family.
447. Carrying your child in your belly, feeling their

warmth and kicks under your hands.

448. My parents love me.

449. My parents are proud of me.

450. My parents are supportive of all my decisions.

451. My parents accept me for who I am.

452. My parents accept the way I choose to live.

453. My parents support the way I choose to live.

454. Spending time with a pet.

455. Finding out that you are pregnant.

456. Making a baby registry.

    a. What baby products would you put on your baby registry?

_____

_____

457. Baby showers.

458. Having an easy and smooth experience with your pregnancy and childbirth.

459. I am so grateful for my baby boy(s).

460. I am so grateful for my baby girls(s).

461. I am so grateful for my babies.

462. It brings me such joy to see my baby smile.

463. It brings me such joy to hear my baby laugh.

464. It brings me such joy when my baby looks into my eyes.

465. It brings me such joy when my baby wraps his/her tiny fingers around mine.
466. It brings me such joy to hold my baby.
467. It brings me such joy to kiss my baby.
468. I am so grateful for my children.
469. I thank God that my children are well behaved.
470. I believe that my children are brilliant and talented and for that I am grateful.
471. The first time you hold your niece or nephew.
472. The first time you hold your child.
473. The first time your baby walks.
474. The first time your baby crawls.
475. The first time you hold your grandchild.
476. Becoming a mother.
477. Becoming a father.
478. The calm, still joy of nursing your newborn baby or feeding them the bottle.
479. Becoming a grandparent.
480. Hugging your mother, father, sister, brother, grandmother, grandfather, cousin, uncle or aunt.
    a. It is important to appreciate having the ability to embrace our loved ones while they are still with us. This way we can attract more embraces with them and perhaps more time.

481. Giving your child a bubble bath.
482. Watching your tiny baby play and learn to move around.
483. When your baby smiles back after you give him a smile.
484. When your baby starts sleeping through the night.
    a. This affirmation is great for parents who don't get much sleep.
485. The first time your baby laughs hysterically.
486. When your baby squeals in delight.
487. When your baby babbles so sweetly.
488. Visiting family and friends.
    a. Which family members or friends do you love visiting?

    _____

    _____

489. Reuniting with a family member.
490. Going to High Tea with your mom and sisters.
491. The first time you take your child to Disneyland; taking your children to Disneyland.
492. The first time you take your child to the zoo; taking your children to the zoo.
493. Taking your children and family to apple orchards and pumpkin patches in the fall.

494. Cuddling with your little ones.
495. Going to the beach with family and splashing in the waves together.
496. The grace of having a little person around who absolutely adores you unconditionally; the unconditional loyalty and love your children have for you.

What are some of your own, personal happy thoughts about your family?

5

HAPPY THOUGHTS ON LOVE

IF YOU ARE in search of love, or have already found it, this chapter will be very beneficial for you. It will assist you in attracting more love and romance into your life. It will provide you with the healthy thoughts you need to be thinking in order to draw a healthy romantic relationship into your life.

Repeat these affirmations daily to yourself, and don't forget to act, speak and feel as if you have already found a love. Have conversations with yourself as if you were speaking with a newfound love. Think of what you would like to hear your love say to you and respond as if it were a real conversation. Listen to love songs in dedication to that special someone, whether you've met them or not, and envision what the perfect partner would look like for you. Visualize being with the person of your dreams. This will help you feel as if it were really happening right now, therefore attracting love into your life. Remember, the mind does not distinguish between what is real life and what is in your mind unless you decide for it to do so.

This chapter also includes affirmative thoughts about your partner or the type of partner you seek. These thoughts are directed towards those who have struggled with relationships in the past because they have maintained a negative mindset about their partners and previous partners. It will assist you in thinking better of your significant other and perhaps eliminate some dysfunctional perceptions and generalizations you may have concerning them. For example, some women tend to think that all men are emotionless and insensitive, therefore they draw more emotionless, insensitive men into their lives, and the law of attraction reflects back to them their dominant thoughts. They continuously find themselves dating insensitive and emotionless men and can't understand why the pattern continues. It is because they focus on the negative attributes of the men they date. This chapter will teach you how to draw in the type of

Hamad

partner you desire and provide you with the healthy thoughts you need to be thinking in order to do so.

If you have a love in your life, it is important to practice these thoughts as gratitude in order to maintain this healthy, functional, loving relationship you have. The more grateful you are for each beautiful aspect about this relationship, the more it will continue to flourish.

497. I am so grateful to have a partner who wants to protect me.
498. I am so grateful to have a partner who is affectionate.
499. I am so grateful to have a partner who shows me gratitude.
500. I am so grateful to have a partner who is caring.
501. I am so grateful to have a partner who is responsible.
502. I am so grateful to have a partner who is cooperative.
503. I am so grateful to have a partner who is logical.
504. I am so grateful to have a partner who is reasonable.
505. I am so grateful to have a partner who is intelligent.
506. I am so grateful to have a partner who is spiritually well.
507. I am so grateful to have a partner who is brave.
508. I am so grateful to have a partner who is confident.
509. I am so grateful to have a partner who has a great mind and is a great thinker.

510. I am so grateful to have found a partner whom I am incredibly content with and who is also incredibly content with me.
511. I am so grateful to have a partner who possesses all the qualities I have been looking for.
512. I am so grateful to have a partner who enjoys satisfying my needs and wants.
513. When my love and I enjoy a song together.
514. Finding out that the person you're in love with is in love with you too.
515. The beginning of your newfound relationship.
516. Being in love for the first time.
517. The warmth of holding hands with your love.
518. Butterfly kisses.
519. Hugging your love tight.
520. Forehead kisses.
521. Going hiking with your love.
522. The simple joy and completeness of holding your love's soft hands.
523. Romantic forests with your love.
524. Chin kisses.
525. Hand kisses.
526. Neck kisses.
527. Lying in the sand, holding hands, and watching the sunset on a Caribbean beach with your love.

528. That elated feeling of falling in love.
529. Your first kiss from your love.
530. Missing your love when you're away.
531. Spending time with the person you're falling in love with.
532. Walking through hanging flower gardens with your love.
533. Shoulder kisses.
534. When the person you're in love with says your name.
535. Posing for pictures with your love.
536. Waking up in the morning next to your love.
537. The joy of knowing with full confidence that your love is true and loyal.
538. When your love demonstrates their loyalty to you.
539. Resting your head on the chest of your love.
540. Going to a basketball game with your love.
541. Going to Disneyland with your love.
542. Falling in love with your partner over and over again.
543. Going to the movies with your love.
544. Being on an airplane with your love.
545. The perfect kiss with your love.
546. Cuddling with your love.

547. Going to lunch with your love.
548. Going to an amazing concert with your love.
549. Going on a romantic boat ride with your love.
550. Chinese cherry blossom walkways with your love.
551. Going swimming with your love, enjoying a day at the pool.
552. Seeing your love dressed up and looking great.
553. Playing with your love.
554. When your love randomly tells you how much they love you.

What are some of your personal happy thoughts about your love life or the love you seek?

_____

_____

_____

_____

_____

_____

_____

_____

_____

_____

_____

_____

_____

_____

_____

6

HAPPY THOUGHTS ON MARRIAGE

IF YOU ARE seeking marriage or would like to be engaged, you will find this chapter very useful. It will also be beneficial if you are already married or engaged and it will help married couples improve their marriages and relationships with their spouses.

These are the healthy thoughts you will need to be thinking in order to maintain or manifest a healthy marriage and relationship with your spouse or future spouse. Remember, you'll need to think, feel, act and speak positively about your spouse and your marriage, despite your current circumstances.

If you are seeking a marriage, a great way to act on

this focus is to sleep on one side of the bed as if you already have a spouse who is taking up that space. Clear a space in your home for a lifelong partner, like in your closet or in your bathroom. By doing this, you are opening yourself up to receiving and acting in accordance with your thinking, therefore giving that thought more energy and creating that reality for yourself. Plan special vacations for you and your future or current spouse as if they could happen now. Wear an engagement ring—it doesn't have to be real gold or expensive. Just feel that ring on your wedding finger and know that you are engaged or married.

If you are already married, it is important to be grateful for the marriage you have. Even if you find yourself in an unhappy marriage, you must search for what you have to be grateful about your marriage in order to improve it or in order to find a better partner. If you want to save your marriage, focus on all the good qualities about your spouse. Write them down in a gratitude journal each time your spouse shows you their good qualities. You will see more and more of their good qualities and the bad ones will somehow fall away and will no longer show up in your lives.

555. I am so happy and grateful to be engaged to my soul mate.
556. I am so happy and grateful to be on the romantic honeymoon of my dreams.
    a. Visualize the honeymoon of your dreams. Where would you like to go? Find pictures of your dream honeymoon destination and put them in a place where you spend a lot of time.

    _____

557. I am engaged; I am thrilled to be engaged; I am so happy and grateful now that I am engaged; I thank God that I am engaged.
558. I love my engagement ring. It is perfect. It is the ring of my dreams.
    a. Envision the engagement ring of your dreams. What does it look like? Imagine your loved ones gazing at the ring on your hand in amazement and imagine them telling you that your engagement ring is gorgeous and that it's perfect for you.
559. I am a bride and I am overjoyed.

    a. Visualize yourself as a bride. How do you want to look?

_____

_____

560. I am so happy and grateful to have had the perfect wedding.
    a. What kind of wedding do you want to have? Visualize it.
561. I am so happy and grateful that my family is happy with my fiancé.
562. I am so happy and grateful that my family is happy with my in-laws and that my in-laws are happy with my family.
563. I am so happy and grateful that my in-laws are happy with me.
564. I am so happy with my in-laws.
565. I am grateful that my in-laws respect and value me.
566. I am so grateful to have a fiancé who is perfect for me.
567. I am so grateful to have found everything I was looking for in my fiancé.
568. My fiancé is my dream come true.
569. I am so happy and grateful to have kind, carefree

and understanding in-laws.

   a. Imagine having a joy filled relationship with them.

570. I am so happy and grateful that my relationship with my in-laws is easy, fun and effortless.

571. I am grateful to have a spouse who adores me and whom I adore.

572. I am so grateful to have a partner who is accepting and understanding of who I am.

573. I am grateful to have a spouse who praises me.

574. I am grateful to have a spouse who is interested in what I say.

575. I am grateful to have a spouse who listens to me when I speak.

576. I am so grateful to have a spouse who communicates with me.

577. I am so grateful to have a spouse who is considerate.

578. I am grateful to have a spouse who is a positive person.

579. I am grateful to have a spouse who is proactive.

580. I am grateful to have a spouse who is happy with me.

581. I am grateful to have a spouse who is happy with himself/herself.

582. I am so grateful to have a partner who shows me compassion.
583. I am grateful to have a spouse who is successful.
584. I am grateful to have a spouse who is passionate.
585. I am grateful to have a spouse who loves spending time with me.
586. I am grateful to have a spouse who is understanding.
587. I am grateful to have a spouse who is supportive.
588. When my spouse enjoys my cooking.
    a. Picture your spouse telling you that you are a great cook.
589. I am grateful to have a spouse who shows me appreciation.
590. I am grateful to have a spouse who shows me kindness.
591. I am grateful to have a spouse who shows me love.
592. I am grateful to have a spouse who shows me loyalty.
593. I am grateful to have a spouse who shows me how faithful they are.
594. I am happy to have a spouse who is grateful for me.

Hamad

595. Your engagement party.

    a. What would you like it to be like?

    _____

    _____

596. Buying your fiancé the perfect engagement ring, with your name engraved on the inside.

597. Making a wedding registry.

    a. What would you put on your wedding registry?

    _____

    _____

598. Having the perfect hair-do on your wedding day.

599. Finding the perfect wedding dress and then wearing it on your wedding day.

600. Getting the perfect manicure and pedicure for your wedding day.

601. Having your makeup done perfectly for your wedding day.

602. The perfect wedding day decor.

    a. What would that look like for you?

    _____

    _____

603. A gourmet wedding day dinner.

    a. What would you like to serve at your wedding? Try to think of as many details about the food as possible.

604. Having the perfect invites for your wedding day.
    a. What will they look like?

605. Having your wedding at the perfect venue.
    a. What location will it be at?

606. The perfect music on your wedding day.
607. Taking perfect photos on your wedding day.
608. Having a blast with all your loved ones on your wedding day.
609. Looking back on your wedding day and remembering how happy it was.
610. Going to the movies with your spouse.
611. Spending your evenings with your spouse, in your cozy, clean family room, sitting on your soft, comfy couch, watching comedy, laughing hysterically and eating popcorn together.
612. Going to the gym with your spouse.
613. Celebrating your anniversary.

    a. Think about how you would love to celebrate your anniversary. What would you like to do?

    _____

    _____

614. When your brother and brother in law are good friends.
615. Cooking delicious meals at home with your spouse and then having your favorite desert after.
    a. Cheesecake, Hershey's sundae pie, chocolate chip cookies, brownies, pazookies.
616. Spontaneously going swimming on a warm summer night with your spouse, enjoying the cool water, making jokes and laughing together in carefree spirits.
617. Being on an airplane with your spouse.
618. Hugging your spouse.
619. The perfect kiss with your spouse.
620. Cuddling with your spouse.
621. Enjoying your Jacuzzi at night with your spouse.
622. Being reassured that your spouse truly values, loves and protects you.
623. Feeling safe and secure in your relationship with your spouse.

624. When your spouse tells you how happy they are with you.
625. When your spouse randomly tells you how much they love you.
626. Candlelit dinners with your spouse.
627. Going to lunch with your spouse.
628. Going to a basketball game with your spouse.
629. Coming home to your spouse.
630. When your spouse dresses up for a special occasion and you get to enjoy how attractive they look.
631. Being playful with your spouse.
632. Staying in bed with your spouse.
633. Traveling with your spouse to all the places you've wanted to go.
    a. What places do you want to travel with your spouse?

    _____

    _____

634. Going to dinner with your spouse at one of your favorite restaurants, eating one of your favorite meals.

Hamad

What are some of your personal happy thoughts about your marriage or the marriage that you seek?

7

HAPPY THOUGHTS ON TRAVEL

ONE OF THE most exciting and adventurous chapters of this book, these thoughts consist of some of the most unimaginable places to see in the world, from the Koh Phi Phi Islands of Thailand to the Iguazu Falls of Brazil and Argentina. To all who find themselves desiring to see a certain place in the world, these are the happy thoughts for you. Let your wanderlust loose and feel the excitement of travel rising. You are on your way to the destination of your dreams. See yourself in each of these places or in the places you have been dying to go. Look up photographs of the places your desire to visit and envision yourself being there; put them around your house. You can go any place you would like to go. Plan your trips online exactly the way you would like them to be, as if they could happen right now. Call or visit a travel agent and inquire about this trip you mean to take. Create itineraries for your trip, schedules you would like to have for your trip and write them down. Online shop for the clothes you would like to wear on your vacations. Imagine the foods you'll try. The more passionately you feel the excitement, the faster it will show up in your life.

Also remember to keep record of and practice gratitude the amazing travels you've already experienced. This is how you'll be sure to attract more.

635. I am so happy and grateful that I get to travel the world.
636. I am blessed to live a life of adventures.
637. I thank God for the wonderful vacations I get to share with my loved ones.
638. I am so happy to be able to take road trips with my loved ones and listen to great songs along the way.
639. I am so grateful to be able to enjoy the pleasure of

tasting a variety of delicious foods around the world.

640. I am so grateful to have been to every single place in the world that I intended to go to.
641. Flying first class or private every time you travel.
642. Finally traveling to that place you've been dying to go.

    a. Where have you been dying to go?

_____

_____

643. I am overlooking the Great Barrier Reef of Australia and it is gorgeous.
644. I am enjoying a gorgeous resort in Bedarra Island.
645. I am enjoying the Sea of Stars on Vaadhoo Island of the stunning Maldives.
646. I am enjoying the heavenly resorts of the Maldives.
647. I am observing the stunning views of The Bend in the Yangtze River of China.
648. I am enjoying the beauty of St. Barts Island.
649. I am enjoying the tranquil waters of Whitehaven beach in Australia.
650. I am in the beauty of the Koh Phi Phi Islands of Thailand.

651. I am enjoying the sights and cuisines of Thailand. Bangkok, Chiang Mai, Koh Samui and Phuket.
652. I am in Bora Bora, overlooking the transparent aqua waters, the soft blue skies and woolly white clouds.
653. I am in am enjoying the stunning view of Marian Palace in Turkey.
654. Enjoying the relaxation and pampering of a Turkish hammam.
655. I am overlooking the statue of Christ the Redeemer atop the Corcovado Mountain in Rio de Janeiro, Brazil.
656. I am walking above the clouds in the Yushan National Park of Taiwan.
657. I am enjoying the beautiful sights and nature of Brazil. The Tijuca Forest, The Iguazu Falls and Rio De Janeiro.
658. I am standing in front of the Plitvice Lake Waterfalls in Croatia, enjoying my view of the white foam, the lush vegetation & the soothing sounds created by the falling aqua waters.
659. I am in Italy enjoying Rome, Venice, Sicily, Capri and San Gimignano.
660. I am in Paris, France enjoying the stunning night view from the Eiffel tower.

661. I am in London; I have been enjoying the London Eye, Buckingham Palace and Big Ben.
662. I am in Spain enjoying the Alhambra Palace in Grenada.
663. I am in Spain overlooking The City of Arts and Sciences of the River Turia in Valencia.
664. I am overlooking the stunning La Mezquita in Cordoba of Spain.
665. I am soaking in the bright turquoise waters of Formentera, Spain.
666. I am observing the amazing Mooney Falls of the Grand Canyon.
667. I am enjoying the Havasu Falls of Arizona.
668. I am enjoying the heavenly views of Joffre Lakes, Canada.
669. I am staying at the world's largest underwater hotel in Dubai.
670. I am overlooking the Burj Al Arab in Dubai.
671. I am enjoying the beautiful sights at the Canadian Rockies.
672. I am swimming in The Emerald Pool of Cebu, Philippines.
673. I am enjoying the great sights of China. The Great Wall, Beijing, Jiuzhaigou Sichuanm and enjoying

the delicious Chinese cuisine.

674. I am enjoying the beautiful sights of Budapest, Hungary.

675. I am enjoying New York City at night.

676. I am overlooking the Statue of Liberty.

677. I am enjoying the aqua beaches of Miami.

678. I am enjoying the heavenly views of Opaekaa Falls of Kauai, Hawaii.

679. I am enjoying the bright beaches of Cancun.

680. I am snowboarding in Alaska and staying in a cozy cabin.

681. I am enjoying the amazing views of Niagara Falls.

682. I am enjoying the stunning views of New Zealand.

683. I am riding in a hot air balloon over Napa Valley, California and enjoying the stunning sights of the skies.

684. I am enjoying the stunning transparent waters of the Sand Dunes of Brazil.

685. I am enjoying the stunning green views of the Hawksbill Crag of Arkansas.

686. I am overlooking the amazing Proxy Falls of Oregon.

687. Enjoying the sights of Las Vegas with all your loved ones.

688. Enjoying a luxurious resort in Cabo, San Lucas,

Mexico.

689. Enjoying the El Nido Big Lagoon in Palawan, Philippines.

690. Enjoying the Icebergs Bondi Beach in Australia.

691. Enjoying the amazing greenery Lake Lungern in Switzerland.

692. Going to The Wild Wadi Watepark in Dubai.

693. I am soaking in the Blue Lagoon Geothermal Spa of Iceland.

694. Enjoying the swimming pool balconies at the Aquaria Grande in Mumbai.

695. Enjoying the Hot Air Balloon Festival in Dubai.

696. Staying at the Castle Hotel in China.

697. Enjoying the Amalfi Coast of Italy.

698. Experiencing the Neuschwanstein Castle in Bavaria.

699. Road tripping to San Francisco.

700. Enjoying an infinity pool that blends into lush green mountains and a wide, open sea—a view that seems almost like paradise.

701. Enjoying the amazing rooftop infinity pool at the Marina Bay Sands in Singapore, overlooking the city late in the evening, sipping on fancy fruit drinks with loved ones.

702. Going sailing in aqua waters.

703. The incredible Lake Louise of Alberta Canada.

704. The Hamilton Pool of Texas.

705. I am enjoying Greece and the amazing sights of its many cities. Delphi, Mykonos and Santorini.

706. Staying in the Igloo Village of Finland.

707. Enjoying your very own yacht in aqua waters.

708. Swimming with dolphins in aqua waters.

709. Riding your very own jet skis in aqua waters, the cool air hitting your cheeks and the high of the adrenaline rush.

710. Overlooking the bright colors of the tulip fields in the Netherlands.

711. Going on a jungle adventure.

712. Spending the weekend at a heavenly resort in Turks and Caicos Islands.

713. Spending two full days at Disneyland with all your loved ones and staying overnight at the Disneyland resort.

714. Going on a helicopter ride over an amazing place or city.

    a. Where would you want to ride a helicopter over?

_____

_____

What are some of your own, personal happy thoughts on traveling?

_____

_____

_____

_____

_____

_____

_____

_____

_____

Hamad

8

HAPPY THOUGHTS ON FOOD AND EATING

FOOD MAKES EVERYBODY happy. The purpose of this chapter is to get you excited about food and will most likely have you drooling. But it is also to change the way you approach the act of eating and will encourage you to make eating a spiritual practice.

Our thoughts are very important when we eat. This chapter will teach you how to bring awareness to your thoughts when you eat and how to think healthy as you eat. It will also provide you with the thoughts you will need to practice mindful eating and eating in the present versus eating without awareness. When our minds are consumed by the stress of daily life and when we are not centered, we tend to eat without awareness and eat without enjoying our food. We eat quickly to fill our stomachs and not our souls. What we want to do is become more mindful when we eat, and learn to be "in the now" as we eat. We should aim to enjoy our food as we eat—to chew slowly, to taste and savor our bites of food and to make eating a meditation. This helps lessen the need to eat more, so that we don't overeat. This way, we eat less and eat smaller portions.

It is also important that we learn to think well about how our eating relates to our body weight. To be able to enjoy our food without the subconscious unhealthy background thoughts of: "I am going to gain so much weight by eating this," or "I can't afford to eat this." The focus while eating cannot be weight, because in turn you will attract more weight to your body. The focus should simply be the enjoyment and nourishment of the food; when the thoughts of weight fall away, so will the weight. Envision the food you eat nourishing your body and do not envision the food you eat making you fat or adding weight to your body. See the way the food affects your body in your mind, but see it affect it positively. Envision the food entering your body and supplying it with nourishment, regardless of what it is that you are eating. If your focus becomes nourishment, you will crave more and more nourishing as well as delicious foods and will find yourself practicing healthier eating habits. This is how you can make eating a spiritual practice—by simply being in the moment of it.

In addition, turning to food should not be used as a way to suppress our negative emotions. This is how an addiction to food can be formed. The best way to deal with our emotions is by allowing ourselves to feel them rather than eating to distract ourselves from the pain.

Thinking these thoughts is also a great way to change your overall mood and energy frequency from negative to positive. Sometimes thinking about your favorite foods is a great way to get you excited and passionate and also helps keep you on a positive frequency. Remember, passionate emotions help manifest things faster in your life. And who isn't passionate about food?

However, I recommend avoiding this chapter if you are currently on a strict diet.

715. I am so happy and grateful that I am able to eat the foods that I enjoy eating and still stay healthy, slim and fit.
716. I eat this food with the understanding of the

nourishment it gives my body and the pleasure its tastes give me.

    a. Envision this food nourishing your body as it enters it. Only envision nourishment when thinking of the food you eat and how it relates to your body.

717. I see the nourishment this food supplies my body with as it enters.

718. I thank God for the ability and pleasure of tasting all the delicious foods in the world.

    a. It is important to realize how much of a blessing it is to be able to travel around the world and taste different and delicious foods. When we have the ability to do this, we should savor the different flavors and truly appreciate them and the experience of eating worldly foods. This is how we keep this blessing in our lives.

719. I am grateful that I am a great cook, and that I along with others get to enjoy the delicious tastes.

    a. If you aren't naturally a great cook, this is a great affirmation to use. Especially if you haven't experienced enjoying your own cooking along with others.

720. Enjoying all of your favorite cravings at once.

    a. During mediation, visualize enjoying every single one of your most recent cravings at once. Taste them and chew them in your mind. Very soon this vision will become a reality!

721. Going to The Cheesecake Factory just for cheesecake.

    a. Hershey's Chocolate Bar Cheesecake, White Chocolate Raspberry Truffle, Ultimate Red Velvet Cake Cheesecake, Reese's Peanut Butter Chocolate Cake Cheesecake…the list goes on. Think of your favorite Cheesecake Factory cheesecake.

722. Glass pitchers of chilled water with sliced lemons, limes, cucumbers and strawberries.

723. Thai dinner. Pad Thai noodles, spicy fried rice, sweet grilled chicken skewers, crunchy little egg rolls with sweet and sour dipping sauce.

724. Enchiladas. Drenched in red or green sauce with cheese sprinkled on top and a side of sour cream, lettuce and tomatoes.

725. Burritos. Loaded with Juicey steak, rice, sour cream, cheese, corn salsa and pico de gallo.

a. How do you like your burritos?

_____

_____

726. Tacos. Crunchy with ground beef, cheese, lettuce, tomatoes and sour cream; Warm corn or flour tortillas with fresh carne asada or chicken, pico de gallo and cheese.

a. How do you like your tacos?

_____

_____

727. Quesadillas with juicy steak or chicken, lots of melted cheese, rice, sour cream, guacamole, corn salsa and fresh lettuce and tomatoes on the side.

728. Crunchy tostadas. Filled with steak or chicken, rice and beans, lettuce, pico de gallo, cheese, sour cream and guacamole.

729. Pizza. Cheese, pepperoni, veggie with buttery garlic dipping sauce.

730. Chinese dinner. Chow Mein, crunchy orange chicken and egg rolls.

731. Spaghetti with juicy marina covered meatballs.

732. Creamy ravioli with garlic bread and salad.

733. Lasagna with garlic bread and salad.

734. Cannelloni with garlic bread and salad.

735. Shrimp scampi with garlic bread and salad.

736. Mediterranean dinner. Falafel, hummus, grilled chicken with garlic paste and garlic lemon potatoes with cilantro sprinkled on top.
737. Cheeseburgers with French-fries and your favorite soda.
738. Hotdogs. Onions, ketchup, mustard, relish, mayo, chili cheese or coleslaw.
739. Cheese fries.
740. Nachos. With cheddar cheese sauce, ground beef, lettuce, tomatoes, onions and sour cream.
741. Hot wings.
742. Seasoned curly fries.
743. Sweet potato fries. Crunchy and sweet with ranch.
744. Crispy thin cut garlic Parmesan fries with unique dipping sauces.
745. Sushi with Miso soup and edamame. California rolls, Dragon rolls, spicy tuna rolls and Philadelphia rolls.
    a. What are your favorite sushi rolls?

    _____

    _____

746. Hibachi dinner. With Miso soup, salad with ginger dressing, garlicy fried rice, grilled veggies, fried noodles, New York steak and plump, juicy shrimp.

747. Barbeque dinner. Steak, chicken, fish, shrimp, plump juicy hotdogs, creamy potato salad, sweet cornbread with cinnamon butter and a coke.
748. The simple pleasure of fruits, veggies, and hard-boiled eggs.
749. Creamy macaroni and cheese with five different kinds of melted cheeses, baked to perfection and croutons sprinkled on top.
750. Breakfast on your first day off.
    a. What does this look like for you?

    _____

    _____

751. Cinnamon spice pancakes, cheesy scrambled eggs and a glass of cranberry juice.
752. Steak dinner. With salad, potatoes (Scalloped, mashed or baked and loaded with goodies) and garlic bread.
753. High Tea in the afternoon, with gourmet finger foods, pastries and lovely china.
754. Salmon dinner. With asparagus and scalloped potatoes.
755. Lobster dinner. With a side of butter, seared potatoes, corn, coleslaw and a buttered dinner roll.
756. Soup. Broccoli cheddar, chicken noodle and lobster bisque.

a. What is your favorite soup?

_____

757. Fancy breakfasts overlooking the sea. Waffles, eggs Benedict, sliced fruits and berries, bagels, toast, coffee, juice and sparkling cider.
758. Sparkling colorful drinks with fruit toppings and pretty straws.
759. Colorful salads.
760. Fresh, raw, juice. Apples, Oranges, Carrots, Celery, Cucumber, Spinach, Kale, Parsley and the thought of getting plenty of micronutrients and nourishment into your body.
761. Dessert and candy tables. Licorice, gummies, chocolates, fruit chews, lollipops, cupcakes, cake-pops and little cups filled with pudding and mousses.
762. Fruit and yogurt parfaits.
763. Graham crackers with peanut butter and a glass of apple juice.
764. Grilled cheese sandwiches with tomato basil soup —cheddar cheese, Pepper jack or American.
765. Chicken salad sandwiches on buttery soft croissants with crunchy green onions and red peppers.

766. Italian flavored sodas. Berry pomegranate, creamy strawberry, peaches and cream, cherry lime, coconut and passion fruit.

767. Moist, sweet, fudgy, chocolaty brownies.

768. Hot coco on Christmas Eve; Peppermint, Caramel, Double Chocolate, and Toffee Nut with whipped cream on top.

769. Soft serve ice cream on a big waffle cone.

770. Gelato. Cream, vanilla, chocolate, hazelnut, pistachio, almond, tiramisu, coconut and espresso.

771. The tremendous satisfaction of finally getting that food you've been craving.

772. Having your own garden of fresh fruits and vegetables.

773. Watermelon popsicles with mint.

774. A Chai tea latte, iced or hot.

775. A hot stack of fluffy pancakes, with blueberries, cranberries almonds, drenched in melting butter, syrup and whip cream.

776. The beauty and deliciousness of tropical fruit drinks and smoothies.

777. Disneyland funnel cakes. Crispy, hot, sweet crunch, warm strawberry sauce and powdered sugar melting in your mouth.

778. Crispy Disneyland corndogs with mustard and

ketchup.

779. A buttermilk spice muffin.

780. Coffee. Sweet, strong, steamy, rich, hot, smooth, nutty and fresh.

781. S'mores in your backyard bonfire, with Hershey's chocolate, fluffy marshmallows, crunchy, sweet graham crackers and Recess Peanut Butter Cups.

782. Krispy Kreme Doughnuts. Crispy, warm and sweet, melting in your mouth.

783. Australian strawberry liquorice.

784. Frozen yogurt with tiny soft and sweet gum drops, strawberry bobas, and mangos.

    a. What do you like on your frozen yogurt?

_____

_____

785. Starbucks Frapuccinos. Caramel, mocha, chai, vanilla, strawberries and cream, green tea.

786. Your favorite candy.

    a. What are your favorite kinds of candy?

_____

_____

787. Laffy Taffies.

788. Hershey's Crème Pie.

789. Hot oatmeal with peanut butter, honey and toast

on the side.

790. Every flavor cupcake. Red velvet, double chocolate, coconut, strawberry, white, vanilla, peanut butter, chai latte and toffee nut.

What are some of your own happy thoughts on food and eating?

_____

_____

_____

_____

_____

_____

_____

_____

_____

_____

_____

_____

_____

_____

_____

_____

9

HAPPY THOUGHTS ON MONEY

EVERYONE COULD USE a little more money. This chapter will appeal to all who are seeking a greater financial income. These affirmations will help you draw more money into your life. Doing so is simpler than you might think and that is why these thoughts are so simple. All you need to do is shift your thoughts and focus to having more money. Repeat these affirmations daily to yourself and also feel, act and speak as if you had the exact amount of money you would like to have. Practicing gratitude is also a great way to attract more wealth. Wallace Wattles, author of The Science of Getting Rich, stated: "The daily practice of gratitude is one of the conduits by which your wealth will come to you." In my own experiences, I have found that you cannot attract more money without first being grateful for the money you already have. Keep record in a gratitude journal of all the small and big things you are able to do with the money you already have. Be grateful for every purchase you are able to make and for the money you have to pay for it. Be grateful for every dollar and penny amount you have and be grateful for whatever is the current amount in your bank account. This is how you can increase it.

One great way to act as if you have money is to go online shopping and add everything that you want to your shopping cart. You can even fill out all the check out information (without hitting submit) and really feel as though you are able to purchase all the things you want. Feel as if you are going to be receiving everything you have added to your cart. Start waiting for the package to arrive. Get excited and envision yourself having it all.

When you are alone, celebrate having received all of the money you have desired. Shout, jump up and down, and say things like: "I can't believe it. I'm rich!" Carry in your consciousness the fact that you are as wealthy as you would like to be as often as you can. Go to places of affluence or places where the wealthy go and feel as though you are one of them. Ground your wealth into your subconscious by thinking about it in the morning and at night before you sleep. Remember your wealth as often as you can and soon it will show up in your life.

791. There is an abundant supply of money in the world and I can have as much of it as I want.
792. Money comes abundantly and frequently to me.
793. I am so happy and grateful now that I am financially free.
794. I am so happy and grateful to have financial independence.
795. I thank God for all of this money.
796. I am so grateful to be able to make more than enough money to support my family and myself.
797. I am so happy and grateful now that I am rich.
798. I am set for life.
799. I am so happy and grateful that I have more than enough money to buy all the things I want.
800. I am so happy and grateful for my absolute, perpetual wealth.
801. I am so grateful for the ability to acquire money with ease.
802. I have more money than I ever imagined.
803. I have exactly the amount of money I want to have.
    a. What is the exact amount of money you would like to have?

    _____

804. I am wealthy.

   a. How do you envision your life as a wealthy person?

805. I am so happy and grateful to have the money to buy all the things I've wanted.

806. I am so grateful to be making _____ dollars every month.

807. I am so grateful to be making _____ dollars a year.

808. I am so happy and grateful to have more than enough money to do all the things I've wanted to do.

809. I have an abundant supply of money that comes perpetually to me.

810. Winning the lottery.

811. Financial freedom.

812. The world is abundant with money and wealth and I can have as much of it as I want.

813. When your boss calls you in for a meeting and gives you a raise and a bonus.

814. The joy of quitting your job knowing that you have so much wealth that you no longer need to work.

815. The freedom of knowing that you never have to

wake up early and go to work ever again.

816. Having all the money you need to travel.

817. Retiring young; having so much wealth that you have the option of retiring young.

    a. Imagine having so much perpetual wealth that you can retire whenever you want. What age do you want to retire at? How much money do you want to have when you retire?

    _____

    _____

818. Buying the perfect home for you, your dream home. Then walking into it knowing that it's already yours.

819. Buying the perfect furniture for your new home.

    a. What furniture have you been wanting for your home?

    _____

    _____

820. Buying that bike you've been wanting and riding it in every beautiful place you can find.

821. Buying the perfect camera.

822. Buying that huge, ultra high definition TV you've been wanting.

823. Finding the perfect bedding set for your bed and

then buying it without a worry about the cost.

824. Buying the outfit you've been wanting and then wearing it.

825. Buying the most beautiful handbag you've ever seen.

826. Buying the most beautiful necklace you've ever seen.

827. Buying the most beautiful bracelets you've ever seen.

828. Buying the most beautiful earrings you've ever seen.

829. Buying the most beautiful diamond ring you've ever seen.

830. Buying the pair of shoes you've been wanting and then putting them on.

831. Buying the perfect coat.

832. Buying the perfect pair of jeans that fit you perfectly.

833. Buying the perfect collection of makeup.

834. Buying the perfect swimsuit that fits perfectly.

835. Buying the perfect pajamas.

836. Buying the cutest baby outfits for your baby.

837. Buying a Yacht, designed custom for you.

838. Flying on a private jet or first class, knowing you

can continue to do it for the rest of your life.

839. Going online shopping knowing that you can buy as much as you want.

840. Going to the mall knowing that you can buy as much as you want.

841. Going to Target and buying all of your favorite toiletries, knowing you have more than enough money to buy all of them.

842. Taking your entire family out to dinner and the joy of knowing you have more than enough money to pay the entire bill.

843. Buying your mom and dad a car.
    a. Imagine how fun it would be to surprise your mom or dad with a car. What car would you get them? See it and enjoy that moment in your mind.

844. Buying your parents a house.

845. Taking your siblings shopping and buying them whatever they want.

846. Going shopping and buying all of the things you want on sale and at a great price.

847. Starting the business of your dreams.
    a. What would your dream business be?
    _____
    _____

848. The first thing you buy after you find out you are rich.

   a. What are the first things you would buy if you found out that you were rich?

   _____

   _____

Hamad

What are some of your own, personal happy thoughts on money?

_____

_____

_____

_____

_____

_____

_____

_____

_____

_____

_____

_____

_____

_____

10

HAPPY QUOTES BY HAPPY PEOPLE

THIS CHAPTER IS meant to inspire and motivate you. It is a compendium of quotes from some of the most influential visionaries of the past and present. These quotes are great for lifting your spirits when you are feeling discouraged. So, when you begin to lose hope, try reading some of these inspirational statements. As Imam Ali Ibn Abi Talib stated: "Like your body, your mind also gets tired, so refresh it with wise sayings."

849. "Certainly the Lord will guide me where I need to go." ~Mariah Carey
850. "I've been smiling lately, thinking about the good things to come. And I believe it could be. Something good has begun." ~Cat Stevens
851. "There will be an answer. Let it be." ~The Beatles
852. "I'm on the edge of glory." ~Lady Gaga
853. "I know exactly where I'm going. I'm getting closer and closer everyday. And I'm almost there. I'm almost there." ~Disney's *The Princess and the Frog*
854. "I will find my way. I can go the distance. I'll be there someday, if I can be strong. I know every mile will be worth my while." ~Disney's *Hercules*
855. "Follow your bliss and the universe will open doors for you where there were only walls." ~Joseph Campbellc
856. "Go confidently in the direction of your dreams. Live the life you have imagined." ~Henry David Thoreau
857. "Believe you can and you're halfway there." ~Theodore Roosevelt
858. "Your big opportunity may be right where you are." ~Napoleon Hill
859. "Our greatest weakness lies in giving up. The most

certain way to succeed is always to try just one more time." ~Thomas A. Edison

860. "We do not see things as they are. We see them as we are." ~The Talmud

861. "Happier thoughts lead to essentially a happier biochemistry." ~Dr. John Hagelin

862. "You create your own universe as you go along." ~Winston Churchill

863. "Everyone visualizes whether he knows it or not. Visualizing is the great secret of success." ~Genevieve Behrend

864. "The daily practice of gratitude is one of the conduits by which your wealth will come to you." ~Wallace Wattles

865. "Many people who order their lives rightly in all other ways are kept in poverty by their lack of gratitude." ~Wallace Wattles

866. "Whatever we think about and thank about we bring about." ~Dr. John Demartini

867. "Gratitude is absolutely the way to bring more into your life." ~Marci Shimoff

868. "All that we are is a result of what we have thought." ~Buddha

869. "That a man can change himself & master his own

destiny is the conclusion of every mind who is wide awake to the power of right thought." ~Christian D. Larson

870. "Take the first step in faith. You don't have to see the whole staircase. Just take the first step." ~MLK

871. "Thought impregnated with love becomes invincible." ~Charles Haanel

872. "At any given moment you have the power to say: 'This is not how the story is going to end." ~Unknown

873. "One touch of God's favor can trump 20 years of hard labor!" ~Dr. Murdoch Dali

874. "When it is dark enough, you can see the stars." ~Ralph Waldo Emerson

875. "We are shaped by our thoughts; we become what we think. When the mind is pure, joy follows like a shadow that never leaves." ~Buddha

876. "There is no disease that God Almighty has created, except that He also has created its treatment." ~The Prophet Muhammad (Bukhari)

877. "Be merciful to those who are on earth so that the One Who is in Heaven will have mercy on you." The Prophet Muhammad (Tirmidhi)

878. "He who is not merciful to others, will not be treated mercifully." ~The Prophet Muhammad

(Bukhari)

879. "Do not despair of God's mercy; He will forgive you of all your sins." ~Quran (39:53)

880. "And your Lord says, 'Call on me, I will answer you (your prayer)." ~Quran (40:60)

881. "And in God let the believers put their trust." Quran (14:11)

882. "God will aid a servant of His so long as the servant aids his brother." ~The Prophet Muhammad (Bukhari)

883. "The Lord will make Perfect that which concerns me." ~Psalm 138:8

884. "Your Lord will spread for you of His mercy and will prepare for you a pillow in your plight." ~Quran (18:16)

885. "There is a reward for benevolence shown towards any creature." ~The Prophet Muhammad

886. "Verily never will God change the condition of a people until they change what is within themselves." ~Qur'an (13:11)

887. "All that you are fearing is an illusion. F E A R = (F)alse (E)vidence (A)ppearing (R)eal." ~Reverend Run

888. "Forgiveness is giving up hope that the past could

have been any different." ~Tyler Perry

889. "Forgive him who wrongs you; join him who cuts you off; do well to him who does evil to you." ~The Prophet Muhammad

890. "It is impossible to live without failing at something, unless you live so cautiously that you might as well not have lived at all – in which case, you fail by default." ~JK Rowling

891. "The only way to achieve the impossible, is to believe it is possible." ~Charles (Alice in Wonderland)

892. "God would never leave your faith to waste; indeed God is gentle towards the people and compassionate." ~Quran (2:143)

893. "Know that whatever missed you, couldn't have happened to you; and that whatever happened to you, couldn't have missed you." ~The Prophet Muhammad (Tirmidhi)

894. "He who has intended a good deed and has not done it, God records it with Himself as a full good deed." ~The Prophet Muhammad (Bukhari)

895. "Leave that which makes you doubt for that which does not make you doubt." ~The Prophet Muhammad (Tirmidhi)

896. "In Paradise, there are blessings that no one has

ever seen, has ever heard, or can ever imagine."
~The Prophet Muhammad (Muslim)

897. "All that I have seen teaches me to trust the Creator for all that I have not seen." ~Ralph Waldo Emerson.

898. "If daily you feel a sense of gratitude for the blessings of this life it will be a cushion and buffer when challenges arise." ~Rose W-T

899. "Reality is wrong. Dreams are for real." ~Tupac Shakur

900. "Before you can win, you have to believe you are worthy." ~Mike Ditka

901. "What God intended for you goes far beyond anything you can imagine." ~Oprah Winfrey

902. "Only passions, great passions, can elevate the soul to great things." ~Denis Diderot

903. "God wishes to make things easy for you and not to make things difficult for you." ~Quran (2:185)

904. "Sometimes when things are falling apart, they may actually be falling into place." ~Marilyn Monroe

905. "If you put your trust in God in the true sense, He will grant your provision as He grants to the birds, who go out in the morning hungry and come back

full." ~Ahmad, Ibn Maajah and al-Tirmidhi

906. "Be thankful for what you have; you'll end up having more. If you concentrate on what you don't have, you will never, ever have enough." ~Oprah Winfrey

907. "God is kinder than you think." ~Reverend Run

908. "You'll never rise any higher than the way you see yourself." ~Joel Olsteen

909. "We exist in each other as thoughts." ~Deepak Chopra

910. "When everything seems to be going against you, remember that the airplane takes off against the wind, not with it." ~Henry Ford

911. "God will not call you to account for thoughtlessness in your oaths, but for the intention in your hearts." ~Quran (2:225)

912. "The most rewarding things you do in life are often the ones that look like they cannot be done." ~Arnold Palmer

913. "Now is the moment that never ends." ~Deepak Chopra

914. "If you don't have a vision, you're going to be stuck in what you know. And the only thing you know is what you've already seen." ~Iyanla Vanzant

915. "Worry is a down payment on a problem you may never have." ~Joyce Meyer

916. "If you don't risk anything, you risk even more." ~Erica Jong

917. "It is not joy that makes us grateful. It is gratitude that makes us joyful." ~David Rast

918. "The best way to disarm your enemies is to increase their capacity for well being and joy." ~Deepak Chopra

919. "Happiness is in the heart, not in the circumstances." ~Unknown

920. "The thing you fear most has no power. Your fear of it is what has the power." ~Oprah Winfrey

921. "We are what we think. All that we are arises with our thoughts. With our thoughts, we make the world." ~Oprah Winfrey

922. "The vibrations of mental forces are the finest and consequently the most powerful in existence." ~Charles Haanel

923. "Asking the right question—not why is this happening, but what is this here to teach me?—puts you in the place to get the lesson you need." ~Oprah Winfrey

924. "Imagination is everything. It is the preview of

life's coming attractions." ~Albert Einstein

925. "Saving one human life is like saving all of humanity." ~Quran (5:32)

926. "I trust God with my Life... after all He gave it to me." ~Oprah Winfrey

927. "Too many of us are not living our dreams because we are living our fears." ~Les Brown

928. "When you believe in a thing, believe in it all the way, implicitly & unquestionably." ~Walt Disney

929. "Whatever the mind of man can conceive, it can achieve." ~ W. Clement Stone

930. "When we're truly present, we recognize the "ordinary" moments are life's greatest gifts. Appreciate the sacred in the ordinary." ~Oprah Winfrey

931. "There is a vision for my life that is greater then my imagination can hold." ~Oprah Winfrey

932. "Indeed if you are grateful, I will give you more and more." ~Quran (14:7)

933. "Don't let the noise of others' opinions drown out your own inner voice. And most important, have the courage to follow your heart and intuition. They somehow already know what you truly want to become. Everything else is secondary." ~Steve Jobs

934. "When you think you can't, revisit a previous triumph." ~Jack Canfield.

935. "When you have inspired thought, you have to trust it, and you have to act on it." ~Jack Canfield.

936. "When people start focusing on what they want, what they don't want falls away." ~Jack Canfield.

937. "No soul knoweth what is kept hidden for them of joy, as a reward for what they used to do." ~Quran, (32:17)

938. "We cannot control other people. Often times you give others the opportunity to create your happiness. And many times, they fail to create it the way you want it. Why? Because only one person can be in charge of your joy, of your bliss, and that's you. Even the people closest to you, they do not have the power to create your happiness. Your joy lies within you." ~Lisa Nicols in The Secret

939. "You will only receive what you intend." ~The Prophet Muhammad (Bukhari)

940. "Nothing turns trials into blessings and sorrow into happiness like a good assumption of God's plan." ~Suhaib Webb

941. "Whoever returns to Me, I accept him no matter

how far he is; and whoever turns away from Me, I approach him and call on him." ~God Almighty (Hadith Qudsi)

942. "Whoever thanks Me, I grant him more blessings." ~God Almighty (Hadith Qudsi)

943. "I am as My servant's opinion of me. I am with him when he makes mention of Me. If he makes mention of Me to himself, I make mention of him to Myself; and if he makes mention of Me in an assembly, I make mention of him in an assembly better than it. And if he draws near to Me an arm's length, I draw near to him a fathom's length. And if he comes to Me walking, I go to him at speed." ~God Almighty (Hadith Qudsi, Bukhari)

944. "There are far better things ahead than any we leave behind." ~C.S. Lewis

945. "There are two ways to live your life. One is as though nothing is a miracle. The other is as though everything is a miracle." ~Albert Einstein

946. "At first glance, it may appear too hard. Look again. Always look again." ~Mary Anne Rodmacher

947. "Your Lord has neither abandoned you nor is he displeased with you." ~Quran (93:3)

948. "If you have faith when you pray, you will be

given whatever you ask for." ~The Bible (Matthew 21:12)

949. "As a man thinks in his heart, so he is." ~The Bible (23:7)

950. "Therefore be patient; surely, the promise of God is true, and let not those who have no certainty hold you in light estimation." ~Quran (30:60)

951. "So lose not heart, nor fall into despair, for you will be superior if you are true in faith." ~Quran (3:139)

952. "We would accomplish many more things if we did not think of them as impossible." ~Vince Lombardi

953. "I was once asked why I don't participate in anti-war demonstrations. I said that I will never do that, but as soon as you have a pro-peace rally, I'll be there." ~Mother Theresa

954. "Impossible is just a big word thrown around by small men who find it easier to live in the world they've been given than to explore the power they have to change it. Impossible is not a fact. It's an opinion. Impossible is not a declaration. It's a dare. Impossible is potential. Impossible is temporary. Impossible is nothing." ~Muhammad Ali

955. "Start with the end in mind." ~Stephen R Covey
956. "You are today where your thoughts have brought you; you will be tomorrow where your thoughts take you." ~James Allen
957. "What you seek is seeking you." ~Rumi
958. "The secret to success is learning to go from failure to failure without loss of enthusiasm." ~Winston S. Churchill
959. "There are extraordinary things in your everyday lives. There are hidden treasures in familiar shadows." ~Unknown
960. "It is not how much we have, but how much we enjoy, that makes happiness." ~Charles Spurgeon
961. "Only your fear causes you to forget that a positive outcome can be realized in any situation." ~Paul Ferrini
962. "Ask and it will be given to you; seek and you will find." ~Matthew (7:7)
963. "Contentment makes poor men rich. Discontentment makes rich men poor." ~Reverend Run
964. "God is the guardian of those who believe. He brings them out of the darkness into the light." ~Quran (2:257)
965. "The way we choose to see the world creates the

world we see." ~Barry Neil Kauffman

966. "Keep praying for what it is you seek. Impossibility and possibility are merely concepts of your mind. To God nothing is impossible." ~Imam Ali

967. "The only way to do great work is to love what you do. If you haven't found it yet, keep looking. Don't settle." ~Steve Jobs

968. "The most common way people give up their power is by thinking they don't have any." ~Alice Walker

969. "You can do anything if you have enthusiasm. Enthusiasm is the yeast that makes your hopes rise to the stars." ~Henry Ford

970. "I've missed more than 9,000 shots in my career. I've lost almost 300 games. 26 times, I've been trusted to take the game winning shot and missed. I've failed over and over and over again in my life. And that is why I succeed." ~Michael Jordan

971. "Faith and fear have a lot in common; they both demand you believe in something you cannot see." ~Bob Proctor

972. "The future belongs to those who believe in the beauty of their dreams." ~Eleanor Roosevelt

973. "Sometimes you just have to believe. To be certain without reason, to have faith in the unseen." ~Liz Betrey

974. "Your happiness is your gift to your family." ~Dr. Robert Holden

975. "Your living is determined not so much by what life brings to you as by the attitude you bring to life; not so much by what happens to you as by the way your mind looks at what happens." ~John Homer Miller

976. "God never tells you to figure everything out. He says if you believe, all things are possible." ~Joel Osteen

977. "If you're not happy where you are, you probably wont get to where you want to be. ~Joel Osteen

978. "God meets you at the level of your expectations. If you don't expect much, if you pray little, you believe little, you're going to receive little." ~Joel Osteen

979. "Since I learned that He longs for me, longing for Him never leaves me for an instant." ~Llewellyn Vaughan-Lee

980. "If the present moment has peace and joy and happiness, then the future will have also." ~Thich Nhat Hanh

981. "Let yourself be silently drawn by what you really love. It will not lead you astray." ~Rumi
982. "The future belongs to those who see possibilities before they become obvious." ~John Scully
983. "Belief is transduced into the biology through the cell membrane." ~ Dr. Christiane Northrup
984. "Belief trumps genes." ~ Dr. Christiane Northrup
985. "Find a place where there's joy and the joy will burn out the pain." ~Joseph Campbell
986. "In life we don't get what we deserve all the time. We get what we expect." ~Robert Grant
987. "Whatever your powerful mind believes will come to pass." ~Paramhansa Yogananda
988. "And when you have decided, then rely upon God. Indeed, God loves those who rely [upon Him]." ~Quran (3:159)
989. "Give thanks for unknown blessings already on their way." ~Native American saying
990. "I am sure God keeps no one waiting unless He sees that it is good for him to wait." ~C.S. Lewis
991. "Never go to sleep without a request to your subconscious." ~Thomas Edison
992. "I don't believe that the future is set in stone; I think we have some degree of influence over it."

~Tyler Henry

993. "Needing nothing attracts everything." ~Russell Simmons

994. "If a blessing descends upon you, then make it last by being grateful." ~Imam Ali

995. "Even the smallest of things that you do blossom and multiply far beyond you. A kindness, for instance, may triple for days or set things in motion in different ways." ~Nancy Tillman, *You're Here for a Reason.*

996. "Don't worry about failures, worry about the chances you miss when you don't even try." ~Jack Canfield.

997. "There are gifts to be found in everything, even if those gifts are simply the lessons we learn from difficult situations and people. We find miracles when we look for what is right." ~Melody Ross, *Choose Happy*

998. "Don't put out a catcher's mitt. Step aside, beautiful friend, and let it go right past you." ~ Melody Ross, *Choose Happy*

999. "Everyone has been made for some particular work and the desire for that work has been put in every heart." ~Rumi

1000. "Let the beauty of what you love be what you

do." ~Rumi

1001. "Anyone who genuinely and consistently with both hands looks for something, will find it." ~Rumi

Hamad

What are some of your own, favorite happy quotes?

_____

_____

_____

_____

_____

_____

_____

_____

_____

_____

_____

_____

_____

_____

_____

Hamad

ABOUT THE AUTHOR

Hanaa Hamad is a mother, writer, teacher and an MFA graduate from the University of California, Riverside. She also received her undergraduate degree in Creative Writing at the University of California, Riverside. Hanaa is deeply passionate about the study of happiness and spiritual philosophy. She teaches spiritual well-being and healthy thinking and writes for her blog at:

www.hanaahamad.com